# THE WRITER IN AMERICA

VAN WYCK BROOKS *has written:*

MAKERS AND FINDERS: A History of the Writer in America,
    1800-1915
  I. THE WORLD OF WASHINGTON IRVING
  II. THE FLOWERING OF NEW ENGLAND
  III. THE TIMES OF MELVILLE AND WHITMAN
  IV. NEW ENGLAND: INDIAN SUMMER
  V. THE CONFIDENT YEARS: 1885-1915
OPINIONS OF OLIVER ALLSTON

THE LIFE OF EMERSON

THE ORDEAL OF MARK TWAIN

THE PILGRIMAGE OF HENRY JAMES

EMERSON AND OTHERS

THREE ESSAYS ON AMERICA: America's Coming-of-Age,
    Letters and Leadership, The Literary Life in America
SKETCHES IN CRITICISM

A CHILMARK MISCELLANY

THE WRITER IN AMERICA

# THE WRITER
## IN
## AMERICA

BY

VAN WYCK BROOKS

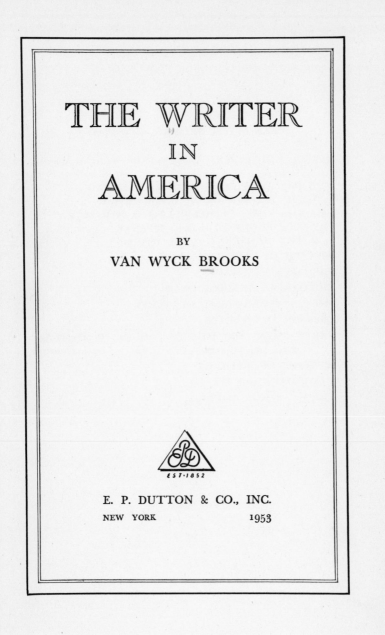

EST·1852

E. P. DUTTON & CO., INC.
NEW YORK   1953

LIBRARY OF CONGRESS CATALOG CARD NUMBER: 52–12597.

To

G. R. B.

## *NOTE*

THE purpose of this little book was, in the first instance, to explain my reasons for writing *Makers and Finders: A History of the Writer in America, 1800-1915*. But, undertaking this, I soon found that my theme required the statement of a certain philosophy of both life and letters.

# CONTENTS

# THE WRITER IN AMERICA

# CHAPTER I

## ON CERTAIN CRITICS

WHEN, SOME YEARS AGO, I began to publish a series of books concerning American literature and its "Makers and Finders," I was taken to task by various critics for calling it a literary history or at least for using this phrase in connection with it. I was told that a true literary history is a history of literary forms, and for this and other reasons I abandoned the phrase. It seemed to me that I had as it were invented a form of my own; I saw no reason to challenge competition, and, having a specific aim in writing the series in question, I found a more suitable title that made this clear.

What struck me at the time, however, was the strangely dogmatic assumption that one type of literary history alone is "true," for literary history has varied in the past like ordinary history and might have had its Herodotus with its Ticknor and Taine. Differing times and differing conditions produce the need of differing types in this as in every other department of writing, and a literary history confined to "forms" would perpetuate the fallacy that books breed books by a sort of immaculate conception. In reality books are bred by men, men by life and life by books through a constant interrelation and cross-fertilization, so that an element of social history can scarcely be dispensed with in any account of literary phenomena and forces. Why were novels, a century and a half ago, so often written in the form of letters, as one sees in the case of our novelist Charles Brockden Brown? One cannot answer this simple question unless one knows something of the part that letter-writing played in the life of that time, in the youth, for instance, of Martha Jefferson or Theodosia Burr, who might have been friends of the heroines of Brockden Brown's novels. When one knows something of the conscious care with which young ladies of that generation were instructed in the art of letter-writing, —with the art of the guitar, the harpsichord, the singing of ballads,—only then can one understand how natural it was that novels should have been written in the form of letters. Especially in dealing with American literature an exclusive preoccupation with forms would produce, it seems to me, the unhappiest results, because in our brief history the inventors of forms have been few indeed and most of our writers have been derivative in this aspect of their work. In a history of literary forms in America much might be said of Whitman and Poe, but what could be said, for example, of Fenimore Cooper? One could hardly find a word to say about this writer who has played a large role in the American imagination.

What this means is that the main interest of American literature resides in other aspects than the purely aesthetic, although I am well aware of the dangerous implications of what once would have appeared an obvious remark.* Let me repeat for the moment here Björnstjerne Björnson's observation, about Norwegian literature, to George Brandes, the critic, that he would benefit no one greatly if, with his "absolute beauty worship," he were to "traverse our little literature." What Björnson meant was that no purely aesthetic criticism could adequately measure the strength of the literature of Norway, which was so largely a *Heimatkunst,* as the Germans used to say, a "homeland-art" with slender aesthetic pretensions. This literature, nevertheless, was important to Norwegians, just as American literature is important to us, and we know that a purely aesthetic criticism would exclude not only Fenimore Cooper but others who are not merely "homeland" writers. For one, there is Theodore Dreiser, a novelist of breadth and depth, who has always been the despair of aesthetic critics. In any case, what reason is there for restricting literary history,—any more than other kinds of writing,—to a single type? Why not think rather of the variety of its possible forms, the four types, for example, which the eminent critic Alfonso Reyes has enumerated in a Mexican magazine? I should say more truly that Alfonso Reyes is

* Since I have spoken of Fenimore Cooper, may I ask what is the implication of Wyndham Lewis's reference to him in *Rude Assignment?* Lewis speaks of Fenimore Cooper as "one of the least adroit novelists who ever won lasting fame." That a novelist lacking in adroitness *could* win lasting fame is a paradox from the point of view of the aesthetic critic, yet how often some such phrase might be repeated in connection with our writers.

quoting Jules Romains in a series of lectures delivered
in Mexico City,—lost now, perhaps, for the lectures
were not published or written,—suggesting a history of
the opinions of the public, or a history of contemporary success, along with three other types that have not
been exhausted. One, relating the history of literature
as it expresses society, might continue further the
method of Taine, while another might conceive of literature as a special autonomous activity with, so to
speak, extra-social laws. A fourth might see literature
as a succession of miracles, geniuses and master-works,
considered apart from historical tendencies and relations. To these types proposed by Jules Romains one
might add the types proposed by Julien Benda in the
preface to *Belphegor*, in which this French critic cites
various others, one of whom also suggests a literary
history as a history of public opinion. A second observes that the study of public opinion and taste
"should be a part of every literary history," remark-
ing that Lanson frequently expressed this view, and
Benda himself adds, "What a marvellous subject"
would be "a history of the aesthetics of French society." But one could add indefinitely to these suggestions.

To insist then that a literary history must be a
history of literary forms is merely to express,—is it not?
—a fashion of the moment, but one that has acquired,
with the school of critics that has given birth to this
idea, a singular hold upon academic circles. It is true
that fashions always change, as conceptions of history
are constantly changing, as they changed with the

minds of Seeley and Acton, the professors of history at Cambridge whom George Macaulay Trevelyan quoted in his Memoirs. Seeley told Trevelyan in 1893 that Carlyle and Macaulay were "charlatans," for history was a science and literary qualities were wholly extraneous to it, while Lord Acton, shortly afterward, told him just the opposite,—Macaulay, on the whole, was the greatest of historians, he said. But as long as the Seeleys are in control, the Macaulays are always in disrepute, and, while our dominant critical school does not insist on "science," it is concerned with "art" in one aspect only. The motto of this school might be "In craft all values lie,"—a phrase of one of its best practitioners,—and its sole interest is literary form, which naturally leads to the notion of a literary history in harmony with this prepossession. Meanwhile, the writers of this school have become our critical "policy-makers," to use a political phrase in this other sphere.

That questions of literary form are vital no serious writer would ever deny,—one could challenge this interest only in the matter of degree, not to gainsay the importance of form but rather to bring forward what else of importance this interest fails to consider. The friends of the "new" criticism, if one may so describe them,—though the phrase has lost its freshness and the friends are not all friends,—the protagonists of the critical movement of the last two decades have reaped the fruits of their obvious literary virtues. One can understand the honest pride of John Crowe Ransom introducing a recent collection of their critical essays, for several of the essayists are admirable writers, with subtle minds and distinguished styles, lovers of literature, perhaps, devotees surely. For them "the wrong of unshapely things is a wrong too great to be told" and they have set out to rectify it in literary matters with a rationale of craftsmanship that has gone far to create a mental climate that fosters literary skill. For whatever can be said of contemporary writing, in poetry and fiction at least a certain virtuosity generally marks it, and is this not in large part the result of a critical movement that has focused the attention of writers on technical problems? In advancing the study of aesthetic effect, in setting severe standards, in censuring "passenger words,"—a phrase of T. E. Lawrence, who said he retained "only words that work,"—in fighting against what Leo Stein called the "cant of unreal appreciation," it has added to criticism a formidable dignity and weight. As teachers, for they are mostly teachers, the "new" critics have made a discipline out of what was too often the futility of literary studies, matching with their exegesis and their freight of learning the disciplines of mathematics, philology and science. That they have professionalized criticism, as John Crowe Ransom says,—an art that was formerly in the hands of "amateurs,"—may well be of dubious value if it is true, and whether "Criticism, Inc." or "Criticism, Ltd." is "what we need," as Ransom says, is surely more than doubtful. But that they have made criticism a power in the literary world is a fact in which serious writers can all rejoice.

This is a palpable fact, indeed, that cannot be ignored or laughed away, though the critics in question lend themselves to satire,* recalling the "hauteurs of the inner circle" and the "sacred language of specialists" that Frank Moore Colby ridiculed a generation ago. Writing in *Imaginary Obligations* about the "dreary schoolmen" who stood for the "scientific criticism" of that primitive day, and asking why their relations with literature were so formal and so strained, he said they should "take a course in Mother Goose." This phrase may appear to be flippant, but it has its profundity, nevertheless, for it leads one to ask why the thinking world rejected in the end the lucubrations of the schoolmen of the Middle Ages. This was because scholasticism had lost its vital function, because logical studies degenerated into logic-chopping and trivial displays of ingenuity, because, in a word, the scholastic mind, losing its sense of the content of thought, was more and more concerned with the shells of form. Has not the same fate overtaken the "new" critical schoolmen? When, in connection with criticism, one hears too much of "symbolic textures," not to speak of "categorical expectation," one feels that

---

* See *A Glossary of the New Criticism*, by William Elton, published in *Poetry*, 1948-1949. It may well have been a unique event in the history of literary criticism when this was seriously reviewed as satire by critics who could not believe it was anything else. Meant in dead earnest, it seemed to be, as Peter Viereck said in *The Arts in Renewal*, a "diabolically clever parody . . . Every poet should read that unbelievably humourless 'glossary' to learn how twenty years of brilliant nonsense have helped to . . . frighten the general public away from both poetry and criticism." Could any actual satire be more effective than this?

criticism itself has followed the path of scholasticism and has travelled too far from its source in literature. These are the exegetical questions that scholars have always relished, the games that learned men love to play but that lead to the "deserts of ingenuity" that Mark Van Doren has characterized in this "faulty science at best" that is "not an art."

Speaking further of "contemporary criticism . . . a house," as Mark Van Doren says, "in which I no longer feel at home," this poet and critic has also observed that it is "doing all it can to arrest the lyric in its flight." I would ask the new critics, in my turn, whether they have not ignored the larger bearings even of their own professions, for they seem never to have asked themselves how far their obsession with form is ultimately good for the writers who produce their texts. "There is such a thing as knowing too much about the technique of an art," AE, George Russell, remarked in *The Living Torch,* "because thinking too much about the technique may act as an obstacle to natural expression." It seems to me that this idea is worth at least a moment's thought, especially when, in *The Garden of Epicurus,* Anatole France, an intelligent man, confirms it, saying, "Poets must not be too keen to argue about the laws of their art, for when they lose their innocence their charm goes with it." These remarks may have small appeal for critics and poets who care as little for "innocence" as for "natural expression" and who are at home in the regions of theory that Anatole France calls "arid" and in which he says they "flounder" when they lose these possessions. But what can be the future of a criticism or a poetry that carry too far both self-consciousness and consciousness of method, inhibiting the flow of the unconscious from which all art springs? It strikes me that even now this criticism in its way retards the proper development of American talents, for it stimulates the cerebral faculties at the expense of the feelings upon which the normal growth of the writer depends. Thus, arresting the lyric in its flight, as Mark Van Doren says, it also arrests the mind from which the lyric issues. There are moments when, thinking of modern poetry in relation to modern criticism, one remembers Dr. Cuticle in Melville's *White-Jacket,* the surgeon who, in his concern to demonstrate his own skill, does not observe that the patient has died on the table.

Do I seem to be merely repeating here what Saintsbury calls the "patter-demand,"—never mind the manner, give us the matter? I do not think anyone would deny the value of technical criticism or the much talked of *explication du texte.* Or the "problems of linguistic purity" in which one critic specializes, or the "direct contemplation of the artistic object." It is only an excessive concentration on questions of form to which I refer,—so "close" that one cannot see the wood for the trees or the tree for the leaves,—together with the effect on writers of a dominant critical "pressure-group" with an almost despotic power in academic circles. This not only tends to impede the natural emotional growth of the writer but it also obscures the fact that "form follows function," a phrase of the architect Louis Sullivan that is no less true in literature than it is in the allied art he had in mind. What this means is that "function creates form," that the means of expression are an outgrowth of what is to be said, whereas, under the influence of the new critics, countless young writers think first of their form and feel they must fit their material to a bed of Procrustes. Regardless of their own temperaments and the visions of life that spring from these, they are positively terrorized into writing as if metaphysics, and the forms of metaphysical poets, were native to them; and who has not heard of the students in colleges who have taken to following Henry James, a model with which they have nothing whatever in common? They suppress all their natural humour and their feeling for the world they know to follow the preordained form of the fashionable master because James, for obvious reasons, is a favourite of the critics. Willa Cather, in her youth, was also drawn to Henry James and wrote several stories in his manner, but, realizing that he was an unsuitable model for her personal vision as well as her field, she chose rather to follow for a while Sarah Orne Jewett. It was then that she began the work for which she is remembered. How many young writers are there now with less than Willa Cather's force but enough to develop a novelist's world of their own who will never be able to enter that world because, in their formative years, they have not permitted their "function" to create their "form."

One might go on indefinitely to mention some of the ill effects of the dominance in academic circles of this school of critics,—who have reasons enough, for the rest, to be proud of their achievement,—among them that, with every year, for all the "close" reading they recommend, there appears to be in colleges less general reading. The age of the new criticism has been, in point of fact, the age in which general reading seems almost to have vanished, although virtually every literate American is now a college man and the new criticism largely rules the college. In this age, moreover, literary opinion seems quite at sea, for was judgment ever wilder in regard to values than when Dickens can be called "decadent" and Emerson a "fraud"? One might as well call the sun the source of darkness. Yet critics can have great names now for whom Poe, as a writer, is "exceptionally bad" and Browning is "so inferior a mind and spirit." We have heard the poems of Matthew Arnold described as "chilblained mittened musings" by one of the most eminent writers of the last three decades, as we have heard Milton called "donkey-eared, asinine, disgusting" by the celebrated poet who "chucked out" Virgil and Pindar. Have we not heard Wordsworth characterized as a "silly old sheep" and Meredith's *Modern Love* dismissed as "the flashy product of an unusual but vulgar cleverness working upon cheap emotion"? That Hemingway is the "most important author" who has lived "since 1616" a well-known writer recently asserted, while another has referred to "the age of Henry van Dyke and William Dean Howells" as if these two writers were equals in ignominy. Most of these judgments come from critics who despise what they call the subjective and who have only scorn for the impressionistic, though nothing could be more impressionistic or more subjective, and one asks what scale of values lies behind them. Would not some of these critics be hard put to it to say why Ronald Firbank is not the equal of Cervantes?

The new critics cannot be held responsible for all the literary sins of the age, but they are scarcely concerned to respond to these questions because, preoccupied with "form," they have little to say about values and less about the weighty affairs of "content." For although, in literary metaphysics, form and content are indivisible,—matter and manner, *forme* and *fonde*,—they are practically separate just as the will is practically free, however conditioned in ordinary metaphysics. "We *know* our will is free, and there's an end on't," said Dr. Johnson, and in this sense we know that the means of expression are distinct from the content of writing or what is expressed,* and who finds any serious concern with the question of what is expressed in the critics who follow Mr. Ransom? Or in much of the writing in England of Mr. F. R. Leavis? When Mr. Leavis says of Gerard Manley Hopkins that he is "likely to prove, for our time and the future, the only influential poet of the Victorian age, and he

---

* This is the practical distinction that T. S. Eliot recognizes in his preface to Ezra Pound's *Selected Poems:* "In some of the verses I believe that the content is more important than the means of expression; in others the means of expression is the important thing; some combine both." Elsewhere, Eliot speaks of Théophile Gautier's "balance of inwards and form,"—another way of expressing this practical distinction.

seems to me the greatest," one finds that this judgment is wholly based on the strength and the subtlety
of Hopkins's imagery and not on anything he "means"
or anything he "says." While this illustrates the dic-
tum that a poem should not "mean" but "be,"—since
"it is never what a poem says that matters, but what
it is," in I. A. Richards's phrase,—it leads one to invoke the name of Homer. For the imagery of Homer
was as strong if not as subtle as the imagery of Hopkins, and yet it is not for this reason that Homer has
survived; and when one asks why Homer has survived
one finds at least one reason in a comment on "modern
criticism" by Paul Elmer More. The "one thing characteristic of it," he said, apropos of Mr. Richards, "is
the complete absence of any search for the meaning of
life"; and is it not obvious that Homer survives because he abundantly rewards this search rather than
for any other reason? But the study of what More
called "aesthetic psychology" naturally thrives among
specialists who delight in the kind of authors that lend
themselves to the methods, the approaches, the technique in which they are skilled, and the more abstruse
these authors are the better from this point of view,
regardless of the light they throw on the meaning of
life.* The specialists relish the ambiguity in which
one critic finds the "core of poetic significance,"—the
"imprecision of meaning" that is, in fact, the "chief

* For these specialists literature consists of a handful of
names, Donne, Melville, Henry James and a few other so-called
"difficult" authors, while they ignore the rest who have not gone
in for Mr. Ransom's "desperate metaphysical manœuvres."

virtue" of poetry for him,—as they rejoice in "categorical" and "multiple-level" criticism and a criticism
that might be "ontological" and is "autotelic." Of
course they take pleasure in struggling with questions
of "psychological structure" and the problem of presenting a subject "without predication," welcoming
obscurity and complexity almost for their own sake,
as a horseman looks for higher and higher hurdles.
But the critics and the poets who debate these themes
lead one back to an observation of John Butler Yeats
in *Letters to His Son*, "My complaint is that all literature has gone over to the side of the schoolmaster
and that it used to be carried on by the boys themselves."

What we have here, in short, is an excess of the
academic, not in the old sense of an enslavement to
convention but in the sense of a remark of the poet
Dylan Thomas on a recent visit to this country. "Why
do so many American poets teach?" he asked. "They
graduate from college, and then they stay in college.
When do they learn anything?" The implication of
this remark may even have ceased to seem obvious
now,—that what a poet *should* learn is to be found in
"life," the life which comes to seem positively vulgar
beside the preciosities that flourish in academic shades
and university sets. What poets *do* learn in the present conditions are just these preciosities,—distillations
of life at a far remove,—owing to what Stephen
Spender calls "the petrifying effects of an isolated culture which has too little communication" with the
world outside. This holds true also of the critics who

share these conditions with similar results in their own adjoining field. It is natural that writers should shrink from life at a moment like our own, when the world is as full of terrors as Columbus's ocean, and it is natural that they should withdraw, not merely for economic reasons, into the safety-zone of the "Department of English." For the universities have become what monasteries were in the dark and hazardous world of the early Middle Ages, and for many life seems too forbidding to be ventured into. Facing insecurity, a prospect of atomic wars and at best the tedious bondage of a bureaucratic present, they can scarcely fail to see as an island of the blest, despite its restrictions and drawbacks, the sanctuary of study. This is all the more natural too among heirs of the "word-revolutionists," a group of writers who formed the contemporary mind and whose interests embraced the linguistics, semantics, psychology and anthropology that have added the charms of complexity to the teaching of letters. A whole generation of writers was ready for Mr. Ransom's creed regarding "close" criticism, "close" talk about "forms," looking to "professors of literature . . . professors of English" to take criticism out of the hands of "amateurs." For criticism "must become," he said, "more scientific," more "precise," which requires the "collective . . . effort of learned persons." It was only a step beyond this to say that Shakespeare was an "amateur" too,—the author of "ill-constructed" sonnets,—because he lacked the "university discipline."

At this point the scholastic mind unites with the

mind of Mark Twain, who said that Shakespeare could never have written Shakespeare because he was an illiterate village boy, a proof that, having too little education, one can overvalue it no less than those who have had in a way too much. Mark Twain overvalued education, as self-made men have often done, when he imagined that a scholar's training was a necessary prerequisite to the writing of Shakespeare, and Mr. Ransom, like many another who values "life" too little, overvalues education in much the same fashion. For both imply, or say, that great writing requires for its production a scholar's training. That something is wrong with this conception the common reader feels at once, and all the more when he considers how little education certain great writers have had even in our time, when education is virtually within reach of all, or how little Yeats had, or Kipling, Shaw, Lawrence, or George Moore, or Melville whose "Harvard and Yale," as he said, was a whaleship. When their work was well constructed, it was because they were craftsmen and not for reasons connected with university living, and when it was ill constructed it showed how far a writer can be a great writer without being a craftsman at all. That their work has often been ill constructed, like Dickens's work or Dostoievsky's, follows from the fact,—or what Melville took to be a fact,—that "all genius," as he put it, "is full of trash." Was not Melville partly right, at least, in this?

But when one speaks of the common reader and what he feels and likes, one takes issue with all the new critics at the very outset, though one has the sanction of Dr. Johnson who said that by the "common sense of readers . . . all claim to poetical honours . . . must be finally decided." Dr. Johnson would not have confined this claim to poetical honours only,—he surely meant literary honours of every kind when he observed that this common sense was to be credited in the end "after all the refinements of subtlety and the dogmatism of learning." Did he not illustrate what he meant in treating the metaphysical poets in his oft-quoted life of Abraham Cowley, those poets who had so much in common with certain poets of our day who are "more desirous of being admired than understood"? Several of Dr. Johnson's phrases, referring to these poets of three centuries ago,* apply as well to their followers in our generation, who have also chosen to wear a deciduous laurel that time is equally certain to steal from their brows. For is it not true of them as it was of Cowley that they have not sufficiently enquired "by what means the ancients have continued to delight through all the changes of human man-

---

* "The metaphysical poets were men of learning, and to show their learning was their whole endeavour . . . Their attempts were always analytic; they broke every image into fragments; and could no more represent, by their slender conceits and laboured particularities, the prospects of nature, or the scenes of life, than he who dissects a sunbeam with a prism can exhibit the wide effulgence of a summer noon . . . Their learning instructs, and their subtlety surprises, but the reader commonly thinks his improvement dearly bought, and, though he sometimes admires, is seldom pleased. . . They were not successful in representing or moving the affections . . . Their courtship was void of fondness, and their lamentation of sorrow. Their wish was only to say what they hoped had never been said before."—Johnson, Life of Cowley, in *Lives of the Poets*.

ners"? In Dr. Johnson's view, the common reader knew these means because it was he whom the ancients both pleased and expressed,—pleased indeed because they expressed this reader,—and it was Johnson's view as well that no writers could endure unless they bore this relation to the common reader. And this relation the new critics totally reject. No doubt they feel that the common reader is not what he used to be, for in our day he lies under the critical cloud that rejects human nature itself as beneath contempt. Does he not partake of what has been called "the corruption of the middle class"?—and the imputation of original sin beneath which he lies in the critical mind supposedly disqualifies even his taste. However this may be, the new critics are alone concerned with Mr. Ransom's "small company of adept readers," while Mr. Ransom congratulates the poets for whom he theorizes because their poetry has "lost its public support." They "have failed more and more flagrantly, more and more deliberately, to identify themselves," he says, "with the public interests . . . as if expressly to renounce the kind of affections which poets had courted for centuries." What they seek now is "poetic autonomy," poetry that is "nothing but poetry" and that "cannot count on any customers except those specializing in strict aesthetic effects." For the modern poet "cares nothing professionally," Mr. Ransom says, "about morals, or God, or native land," and, "disclaiming social responsibility," he is concerned with the possibility that "an aesthetic effect may exist by itself." For a rare example of this ultimate art Mr. Ransom cites a poem by a poet of our day who shall be nameless in this connection, a poem which affords, he says, five supreme aesthetic effects that make one think of these five collocations: rosy chocolate and gilt umbrellas, chophouse chocolate and sham umbrellas, porcelain chocolate and fried umbrellas, mushy chocolate and frail umbrellas, Chinese chocolate and large umbrellas. Mr. Ransom adds, concerning this poem, "The subject matter is trifling." But he seems to consider it, as pure poetry, superior to Homer.

So it is indeed, perhaps, if one's criterion is form alone, abstracted from the human elements that made poets important in the days when they were "bards and patriots, priests and prophets," instead of "apostate" and "illaureate," as Mr. Ransom calls them. That they have ceased to be "keepers of the public conscience" he seems to regret in a measure, but he exults, for all that, in a poetic point of view that cannot be avoided in any case because it is "modern." But what does the common reader inevitably feel about this poem from which all the human elements have been abstracted? Like Leo Stein, he is "perfectly willing to leave that kind of literature" to the few who keenly enjoy it along with the author, for it "does not satisfy enough to be bothered with," while he recalls Santayana's remark that "nothing is more barren than art that is interested in itself rather than its subject." And is this not the whole trouble with the new critics, those for whom literature is nothing but an art and who are interested solely in formal problems? For is it true that literature is nothing but an art? Is there no significance in the old phrase "literature *and* the arts," which seemed to set writing apart from all the others? The name of the National Institute of Arts and Letters is one to which no one objects even today, and if literature had been merely an art, or merely a matter of structures and textures, Plato would never have bothered to banish the poets. Nor would Napoleon, a highly intelligent man, have forbidden Madame de Staël to live in France. In any case, in this feverish study of the *alchimie du verbe,* of structure, texture, "metaphysical strategy" and what not, who asks the one essential question, What makes literature great? And what makes it either less great or nugatory?

What makes literature great, of course, is the quality of its subject-matter,—the permanent important and interest inhering in this,—together with as much formal virtue as the writer is able to compass, though in this he may be, at moments, sadly deficient. Melville was deficient in this more than half the time and Mark Twain at least seven-eighths, and even the greatest works of each, *Moby-Dick* and *Huckleberry Finn,* were gravely defective in their structure. Then, if Shakespeare is an "amateur" because his work is "ill constructed," what is one to say of Dostoievsky? From the formal point of view, Henry James remarked, Dostoievsky and Tolstoy alike were "mere fluid puddings," though as writers both were greater by far than James,* and in fact Dostoievsky's writing was as dis-

* Did not James affirm by implication that his method was only valid when a writer did not have too much to "say"? Ex-

orderly as his life, tumultuous, chaotic and often hasty. Like Dickens, who was equally eager to hold his large public, he resorted without any compunction to the stock devices, along with the loose language, of common fictioneers, as if he scorned "art—art—art" as much as Rudyard Kipling and had never heard of the phrase "artistic conscience." What shall one say, moreover, of such easy-going Philistines,—who have nevertheless been read for a century or more,—as Sir Walter Scott, unquestionably great, who cared more for his position than he cared for his art, and Trollope, who compared himself to an undertaker? Were they not in their form as slipshod as one might expect? But Anatole France observed once that all the great writers had written "bad French" or "bad English," and how many of Balzac's French critics have remarked that he wrote badly without for a moment denying that Balzac was great? Émile Faguet said that he had no ideas, no style, no art and yet that he ranked next to Montaigne, Rousseau and Voltaire, while Brunetière was so struck by the badness of the writing of Balzac *and* Molière that he even evolved a principle from it. He said, *"Mal écrire est une condition de la représentation de la vie,*—one *has* to write badly if one is to represent life"; and one might add the comment of the English-

pounding his doctrine that the novel is to be judged by its *oneness,* he wrote as follows in 1899 to Mrs. Humphry Ward: "The promiscuous shiftings of standpoint and centre of Tolstoy and Balzac, for instance . . . are the inevitable result of the *quantity of presenting* their genius launches them in . . . With the complexity they pile up they *can* get no clearness without trying again and again for new centres."

man C. E. M. Joad that "a work is great when it has ceased to matter that it *is* bad." What avails Edgar Saltus his "style polished and style repolished"? Or of what use now to Henry Harland is the "perfect prose" that he at times achieved? Even if these authors were revived, could they compete for long with Emily or Charlotte Brontë or with *Uncle Tom's Cabin,* structurally lax as these all were, impure in texture and abounding in absurdities and clichés?

It goes without saying that other great writers, from Dante to Jane Austen, are impeccable from the formal point of view, as faultless in their execution as in their vision or their themes they are noble, profound, distinguished, perceptive or what not. But are these always necessarily greater than the others? Are there not "very important chunks of world-literature in which form, major form, is remarkable mainly for absence"? It is Ezra Pound who asks this, the Pound who, long before John Crowe Ransom, proclaimed the supremacy of "art" over "vaticination" and who created a new literary canon consisting of inventors of new rhythms and forms as virtually the only important writers. Pound's "masters" were all technical discoverers, and it was this criterion that led him to chuck out Virgil and Pindar, not to mention Thucydides, whom he ranked as a newspaperman. Proposing an anthology to supplant the "doddard" Palgrave, he said this was to be governed solely by the "inventiveness" of poets, their "contributions to the art of verbal expression," in contrast to the poets and poetry that "Aunt Hepsy liked," as he said that Bach's fugues were "arrangements of sound," that sculpture consisted of "planes in relation" and pictures, quite simply, as "arrangements of colours." In all this Pound followed Whistler, who stated his creed for the plastic arts in calling his "Mother" an "arrangement in grey and black," a phrase that Pound spoke of as "basic" for literature and the arts, far as he diverged from this when he mentioned the "chunks of world-literature in which form, major form, is remarkable mainly for absence." Apropos of Whistler's remark, Swinburne said that Phidias had thought of other things than "arrangements in marble," as Æschylus had something in mind besides "arrangements in metre"; and what else did Pound mean when he continued, "It will take a brighter lad than the author of these presents to demonstrate the element of form in Montaigne or in Rabelais"? Were not Pound's own *Polite Essays,* in which he preached the gospel of form, almost wholly lacking in the virtue that he preached? He frankly said he was "dumping" his notebooks on the public, and no literary essays could have been more chaotic.

Well, then, what produced the force of Ezra Pound's criticism if not the "vatication" against which he preached, the didacticism that he defended in one of his letters, saying, "It's all rubbish to pretend that art isn't didactic"? "Only the aesthetes since 1880 have pretended the contrary," he continued, "and they aren't a very sturdy lot." Pound added, "I am perhaps didactic . . . A revelation is always didactic," he himself being a preacher of poetry as art. And who doubts that poetry is an art?—while it is also the "vaticina-

tion" that Pound attacked with a passion that created
an epoch, a passion that conveyed precisely the "message" and the "vision" which he and his followers
repudiated in the Victorian writers. Was Ruskin more
the schoolmaster or the preacher than he? In short, it
was his power of vatication, with his vitality,—*not*
his "art,"—that carried the day for Pound in criticism,
as they had carried the day for Coleridge, whose *Bio-
graphia Literaria,* that Bible of critics, was totally
devoid of form. But of how many "heresies" does this
dispose?—the heresies of the new critics who possess no
orthodoxy to give these reality or substance,—the
"heresy of the didactic," for one, and the "heresy of
the subject," a notion that has been so injurious to
modern writers. Spread abroad by Valéry, who said
that "the *matter* is of small importance," that "nothing is of any importance but method and form," it
disregards the vital fact in writing that the subject is a
"challenge" which evokes the writer's "response." (To
apply Arnold Toynbee's phrase in this other connection.) For the subject serves as a focus for the writer's
emotions, while providing his "art" with something
to be "interested in,"—the desideratum of Santayana's
phrase; and what this means we can see in the work of
the writers who speak of the importance of the subject
with the greatest contempt. Is not *Hugh Selwyn Mau-
berley* Ezra Pound's most memorable poem? And is
not Allen Tate best regarded as the poet of the *Ode
for the Confederate Dead?* As with Gertrude Stein and
her *Three Lives,* the most notable works of these writ-

ers are those in which the subject is of capital importance.*

This is by no means to deny the value of the "mystique of form" of which Pound and the new critics are not the only preachers, for they represent a world-movement in which an indifference to "content" has accompanied an over-concentration on technical questions. One could give countless examples of this from all the seven arts, with an explanation of the social and moral conditions that have occasioned this over-concentration, while one hopes it will not breed the kind of counter-tendency that effaces, along with the evil, the good in a movement. The new critics have disciplined the literary mind, and this should long profit from their work, although at the moment one mainly feels how this over-concentration has stopped the circulation of the blood in both novels and poems. How empty novels have become, with all their virtuosity,—hundreds of novels, that is, of some pretensions,—and how over-concerned the writers are with the manner that interests the craftsman, how little concerned with the matter that interests the reader. How often are the characters mere "dancing mosquitoes," as Francis Hackett put it, discussing a recent novel in which the writer had produced what might be called a miracle in texture, a novel that was peo-

* When Taine said, "The great question for an artist is to find a subject that suits his talent," he was expressing a classical doctrine; and Taine knew from experience what he was talking about, for he was a great artist as a writer who was also a critic.

pled with the "lost souls" of whom Hackett asked,
"Are these people 'souls' as well as 'lost?' " For why,
if they are not souls, should one read about them?
How many novels are clogged or spoiled by the writer's attempt to outdo all others with unheard of technical devices and experiments in form,—both tiresome
and wasted on meaningless subject-matter,—as thousands of poems have been killed in a similar fashion
or have died as it were in embryo, smothered in words.
No doubt these writers have felt they were yielding as
artists ought to yield to "the fascination of what's difficult,"—Yeats's phrase for Henry James's "only difficulty matters,"—as if it were not ten times more
difficult to find great themes and realize them, to find
great meanings in life and make these clear. As if it
were less difficult to compass "that man's scope," which
Shakespeare desired as much as "this man's art." As if
all the technical devices in the world could have made
a Dostoievsky or a critic like Coleridge or even Ezra
Pound.

So one comes back to the question of content and
what makes literature important or great, whether the
writer is distinguished as a craftsman or not; and
often the great writers are as slipshod and technically rough-and-ready as Ezra Pound, the critic, in his
prose. What makes them great is their imaginative
force, or their moral force, or their panoramic eye, or
the size of the arc of life which they subtend,—A. R.
Orage's criterion of literary greatness,—their passion
for the realities of human nature, or the extent of
their outlook, or the typical or central significance

which their work possesses. The presence of the typical in a novel or story was the critic Belinski's criterion of artistic importance, and in this sense *Madame Bovary* is great because it defined for the first time one of the universal human types. So Chekhov's *The Cherry Orchard* is great because it represented a whole phase of the history of a nation and a civilization. So also, relatively speaking, Willa Cather's *My Ántonia* is greater than any mere transcription from life because the leading character stood for "the country, the conditions, the whole adventure of our childhood," as the narrator put it. Some writers are great because they make life seem important, because they make the game seem worth the candle, because they "speak for life and growth," as D. H. Lawrence wished to do, or because of a certain spaciousness and sweep. One might apply to them all the test of Bernard Berenson, referring to the "spiritual significance" of great plastic artists, observing that they have been not merely men who drew well or painted well but men who have always contributed to "life-enhancement." Because they contributed so much to this, one is not too troubled by the technical defects of *Martin Chuzzlewit,* for instance, or *Wuthering Heights,* any more than the listeners who flocked in Boston to hear Father Taylor were disturbed by his defective grammar a century ago. This "one essentially perfect orator," as Walt Whitman called him,—the prototype of Father Mapple in *Moby-Dick*—moved Dickens and Jenny Lind along with Emerson and Webster, none of whom seems to have been annoyed when he "sometimes lost" his "nominative case," feeling as they did that he was "on the way to glory."

All this would seem sufficiently obvious if criticism, now and then, dwelt on the vital questions of literary value, questions which the new critics are virtually bound to ignore inasmuch as their sole criterion is technical expertness. Nor do they merely avoid these questions,—they positively condition their readers' minds against the literature that fails to pass these tests, against whatever is not technically expert al-though, as Ezra Pound says, this includes "very im-portant chunks of world-literature." And how easily minds are conditioned, how rapidly they adjust them-selves to the kind of approach that characterizes a generation, as the minds of students in colleges now are conditioned against all writing in which form is not the one thing necessary. Thus, for the novelists and poets of the future who are listening to their teachers now, John Donne outweighs most of the major poets, as Djuna Barnes's *Nightwood*, which has no "scope" whatever, outweighs all Balzac as it out-weighs all Dickens. This concentration on the small, moreover, destroys all feeling for the great, in which minds that are so conditioned can take no pleasure, for they stumble over the imperfections of these often careless workmen like a man in a forest who cannot see the sun through the trees. Especially these minds are conditioned in favour of whatever appeals to the academic, the writers who lend themselves to exegesis, the fashionable authors of the present or the past, whether novelists or poets, whom not to know argues oneself unknown. So the larger becomes the popular world-horizon, the smaller becomes the horizon of the literary mind, and lucid writing is dismissed as a kind of merchandizing, while the intelligible becomes the superficial. "Once having become accustomed to the unexpected, we despise the easily guessed," as a recent critic put it, although what is more easily guessed than the Greek and Roman classics which the world will still be reading in another thousand years? As if the "art that conceals art," the clarity, the lightness and the grace that eschew the obscure and ambiguous were superficial! As if the metaphysical were alone profound! As if the "crooked corridors" of the later Henry James deserved more respect than the simplicities of Tolstoy, who tried to be simple because he had much to say. I agree with Clive Bell who said he would write "with all the shallow lucidity of Montesquieu, Hume and Voltaire" if he knew the "secret of their superficiality."

It is, no doubt, both natural and right that the minds of professors should work this way, for they are "men," as Ransom says, "who have aged in these pure intellectual disciplines and cannot play innocent without feeling very foolish." One can only reply to this that the poet who cannot play innocent ceases before long to be a poet; and this is generally true of writers, who should not be professors, for these disciplines too often destroy their spirit. Anyone who remembers the Harvard of fifty years ago, when all the professors of English were men of letters, will recall what they said to the student who aspired to write, "If you wish to write anything but text-books, do not teach!" They knew, as aspiring writers themselves, precisely what they were talking about, though the best of them wished to be teachers rather than writers, which made them the great teachers they occasionally were. But, of course, since writers, obliged to live, cannot live by writing, they are sometimes driven to teach when they do not wish to do so, a necessity that is often a tragic necessity but nothing to make a virtue of,—and why should one base a philosophy of criticism on it? Why should criticism be identified with class-room studies and a discipline that has killed the poet in the man?

But why perpetuate the feud between the professors and the literary men, between town and gown, that began with Mencken, who followed his master Nietzsche, himself a professor? A lover of learning can only impugn professors as a devout anticlerical impugns his priests,—*certain* professors, or certain priests, in certain of their aspects, though these may seem all-important at the moment when he writes. Was it not a professor, Sir Walter Raleigh, who said that "criticism, after all, is not to legislate but to raise the dead"? And did not another professor, E. K. Chambers, say that what made "the history of literature" was "the pageant of genius"? Professors vary like other men, and some of them are "amateurs," in Mr. Ransom's sense, like other writers,—lovers of literature, that is to say, which Mr. Ransom seems *not* to mean, as distinguished from the "professionals" who cannot be "foolish." Are these amateurs in danger of being submerged and lost? Hardly, for will not the world see to it that literature in all its forms,—and criticism as one of these forms,—contributes to life? "Every hero," as Emerson said, "becomes a bore at last." So does every school of thinking that outstays its welcome; and the only real danger is that when "vaticination" comes back again it will leave "art" behind in the dusty rear.

## CHAPTER II

## "MAKERS AND FINDERS"

NEAR OXFORD, on Boar's Hill, at Professor Gilbert Murray's gate, one sees a little sign that says "Please come in and look at the flowers." It struck me, when I observed it first, that this was a not unworthy note for a critic to sound in his writings, at least no more unworthy than the "No Trespassing" signs,—"Keep out!"—one encounters in most modern gardens and many modern critics. The sign at Oxford suggested to me that friendly regard for the human race which is not always discernible in contemporary critics, as it suggested a pleasure in flowers to which one finds few parallels in the feeling that contemporary critics have for books. For do these often communicate felicity or zest? There is, and there should be, of course, no one type of criticism, an art that depends on circumstances for the forms it assumes, forms that vary with the functions it is asked to fulfil and the tasks it is obliged to carry out. Herder's Germany called for a Herder and a Lessing and in large measure flowered because of their work, and small provincial Denmark, to widen its horizon, required the cosmopolitan mind of Brandes. So there are times for synthesis as there are times for analysis, and times and occasions for an

Arnold, an Eliot or a Pound, times too when evocation happens to be called for,—Professor Walter Raleigh's "raising the dead." If one wishes, moreover, to
illustrate Professor Chambers's definition of literary
history as "the pageant of genius," Professor Murray's
invitation is by no means an irrelevant motto for even
the most serious effort of criticism.

But why should one wish to raise the dead? Or
exhibit the pageant of genius? Literature is not a garden, after all, and one must have in mind an aim that
evocation is to serve if this is to count in criticism. As
for presenting the pageant of genius in the old com-
prehensive way that prevailed when "general culture"
was the universal touchstone, this has lost favour in a
time when "we seek to discover our own urgent meanings," as Philip Rahv says, "in a creation of the past."
In our hour of insecurity, the critical spirit tends to
admit only the writers of the past who throw some
sort of light on our personal problems, differing widely
in this way from the spirit that prevailed when the
young grew up in a world that seemed secure. In those
days they read for the interest of reading instead of
reading for corroboration,—to be assured that others
are in the same boat with themselves,—and the adven-
turous exploratory spirit had free range then and lost
itself in byways as well as on highways. With what a
feeling of enchantment, then, young readers forgot
themselves in the worlds of the great novelists, the
great travellers, the poets and the critics who ranged
over the whole face of life in the spirit of Voltaire's
remark, "One should have preferences but no exclu-

sions." In the vast variety of literary types that were spread before them, young writers found their affinities in unexpected corners in a fashion that is virtually impossible now when all but a handful of authors are dismissed as Rimbaud's "antediluvians of art." But it is natural that the contemporary mind, inhibited, anxious and driven, in a world that scarcely knows whether to expect a tomorrow, should have lost its feeling for the breadth and sweep of the humanistic point of view and even come to regard it as unprincipled and foolish. Perhaps it is natural that so many are drawn to the dictatorial mind which says "Thou fool" to the independent thinker, even in the name of one who said that to utter this charge was to place oneself in danger of hell-fire.* For they are too driven to value their independence, and, like all dictatorships, this one offers, for the literary mind, or at least for the academic mind, an end of confusions. But does it not offer this only at a price?—the price of the freedom without which there is no "general culture." Ac-

* "We must remember that all modern critics are judged under the aspect of one of the most aggressive, hardest working and portentous critical movements the history of literature has known, the movement which took its beginnings in T. E. Hulme and has T. S. Eliot as its most notable exponent . . . Yeats, in one of his autobiographies, says that the religious life consists in making all things equal, the intellectual life in saying 'Thou fool.' No criticism has said 'Thou fool' so firmly and finally as this modern movement, and in the light of Yeats's remark it is interesting that it has been allied with religion, that it has had the intention (and sometimes the effect) of making nonreligious and nontheological thought and feeling seem foolish, unprincipled and slovenly."—Lionel Trilling, *E. M. Forster*.

cording to Nicholas Berdyaev, this culture has never existed in Russia because the Russian mind is obsessed with problems and culture is rather an obstacle in the way of their solution. Culture, in any case, solves no problems, immediate or ultimate, which explains why it seems to be dying in our contemporary mind; for, now that this too is obsessed with problems, culture has no more to say to it than it has ever said to the "Russian boy." *

There are, however, certain minds that will continue to think *as if* the world were not in peril of imminent destruction and that look forward with faith to a day when our world-crisis shall have passed and men will regain their equilibrium. Freedom will recapture then its primal value for the mind, just as "general culture" will recover its old magic, and critics will display once more the long-shrouded pageant of genius that seems to arouse so little curiosity at present. Meanwhile, perhaps only a specific aim can justify in our day an approach that strikes so many as old-fashioned, and may I say that I had such an aim in writing *Makers and Finders,* a complex aim that will appear in the following pages.

---

* "There is no general culture in Russia, no cultured society, and almost no cultural tradition. In this matter nearly all Russians are nihilists. Why? Because culture does not resolve any ultimate problems . . . For the 'Russian boy' (a favourite expression of Dostoievsky), absorbed in the solution of metaphysical questions, God, immortality, or in the organization of mankind on a new model, as well as for any atheist, socialist, or anarchist, culture is an obstacle in the way of their impetuous rush towards a consummation."—Berdyaev, *Dostoievsky.*

Regarding the American pageant of genius, the subject of my series, my own feeling has changed in the
course of years, for, although I do not think I have
ever overvalued this, I disparaged it in *America's
Coming-of-Age*. This little book was finished in the
spring of 1914, just before the outset of the first world
war, and, looking back on that time now, I realize that
I was reflecting the point of view that prevailed when
I was in college. For, in their views of American literature, there was much in common between Barrett
Wendell at Harvard, Woodberry at Columbia and
W. C. Brownell, the leading critic. One and all agreed
that America was a "literary dependency" of England, as Brownell said and the others taught and
wrote, and Woodberry observed that we had failed to
produce one poet who was even of the rank of Thomas
Gray. Speaking of the New England "Renaissance,"
Santayana said that it was "all a harvest of leaves,"—
dismissing Hawthorne and Emerson as of no importance, along with Prescott, Parkman, Thoreau and the
rest,—and, while Barrett Wendell could not quite have
agreed with this, he found little that was worth considering outside of New England. For the rest, it was
obvious that Brownell took small pleasure in any of
the "American Prose Masters" of whom he wrote. Re-
acting against the too genial critics who, as he said
rightly, assigned us "great writers on the slightest
provocation," he would not allow real greatness to
Hawthorne or Poe. From the point of view of the
serious critic, America was a Nazareth, as it had been
when Thackeray, visiting the country, told his Ameri-

can friends to think better of their artists, or at least
never to "neglect," never to "forget" the admirable
Trumbull, the painter of whom even Goethe had
spoken well. Trumbull might have stood, in American
minds, for most of the American eminences in any of
the arts. That "we every day too easily undervalue our
own artists" was an old Boston essayist's comment on
this, one that was no less true because it was also the
case that they had been overvalued in less critical
circles.

Such was the prevalent point of view forty years ago
at the time when I myself was beginning to write and
when, like various other Americans of the years that
preceded our second revival, I felt that going abroad
was the way to do it. It did not occur to us that
America was interesting in a literary way, and many
young writers who were convinced that they were going to do great things were scarcely aware that anyone
else had done them. Or that anyone was doing them
even in the present, for when Barrett Wendell, in one
of his lectures, referring to Stephen Crane, spoke of
*The Red Badge of Courage* as "sensational trash," he
was reflecting the hostile indifference not only of the
academic world but even of writers themselves towards
the literature of the country. The writers might have
thought better of Crane, who had had a resounding
success, and they were aware of others like Frank Nor-
ris, for instance, but it hardly occurred to them until
almost up to the first world war that Americans were
doing, or might do, anything important. Or, at least,
important in comparison with writers in Europe.

Edmund Wilson has related how, discovering H. L. Mencken and hearing of two or three other emerging writers, he began to see new possibilities in American letters; and he has described well the outlook of that period as I recall it from a somewhat earlier time: "Between our generation and the Civil War there had extended a kind of weedy or arid waste, when people with an appreciation of literature had hardly hoped to find anything of value growing and when they had tended to be suspicious of anything that did manage to bloom." Regarding the past the teachers were half-hearted, and writers were half-hearted about the present, though a new and exciting age was beginning to dawn.

Now, so far as the American past was concerned, it remained a *terra incognita,* a vaguely foggy wilderness, for American minds, long after the American present had become exciting, partly because the American historians had confined themselves mainly to politics and the literary historians had been either provincial or dull. The most powerful voice in criticism, moreover, at the moment knew next to nothing whatever about this past. Mencken, with a German-American mind that was "frankly against the Anglo-Saxon," was bent, as his followers said, on "liquidating" this; and, besides, the American past had small attraction for a new generation that had sprung largely from recent immigrant strains. In the West, as everyone remembers, in the opening years of the century, the liveliest centres in almost every town, attracting this rising generation, were the socialist locals, meeting-places where the literary young were encouraged to share in discussions of the new European writers who were beginning to be heard of. The leaders were commonly Germans or Russians, immigrant intellectuals of a universally radical cast of mind, and they disparaged as bourgeois nobodies the older American writers except when these were also of a radical cast. Because of this influence, at least in part,—an expression of the *zeitgeist,*—all the young writers were sociologically minded and most of them developed as radicals of one type or another, while generally, whatever their background was, they grew up detached from an American past or any sense whatever of an American tradition. For them tradition of any kind was the "dead hand" of the forward-looking, an "intrusion of the past into our lives," as one of them remembered, like the "garrulous reminiscences of a member of the older generation." * Having "no memories," they had "no doubts," as this recorder says, "with which to criticize the spectacle of this modern world, and instinctively we looked forward into it with confidence and belief. We felt that it was good."

Few generations have been so dumfounded by a turn of historic events as the pre-world-war generation this writer describes, a generation that took the world for granted as a place where one could "go outdoors and play." Seeing this world as a summer world, it was bewildered and lost when the temperature fell

* Floyd Dell, *Intellectual Vagabondage.*

overnight to ten below zero, and this would not have happened quite so catastrophically if it had had "memories" and "doubts." For doubts would have made it impossible to take so bland a view of life, as memories would have prepared it for changes in the weather, though this generation was not unique in losing its way in the cold and the dark or in being misprized and forgotten by an unremembering country. "In America," as Hamlin Garland said, "no man and no thing endures for more than a generation"; and where there is no collective memory, where all thought is for the "here and now," with one vague eye directed towards the future, where the immediate, the pragmatic, is the one universal concern, writers are forgotten like snowflakes when they fall. When certain critics say that Dreiser will not be read in another generation, one asks, But who of our time will be read?—and this is partly because the critics turn talents out of doors when they have passed the moment of their first recognition. Have we not seen Sinclair Lewis tossed away like an old shoe because his work had deteriorated in certain respects?—and have we not seen Eugene O'Neill buried alive in oblivion, scarcely re-examined critically in fifteen years? Has this not been the case also with Robinson Jeffers? Was not Edna Millay ignored or snubbed for a dozen years before she died? Was not her rare lyrical talent dismissed as "shoddy"? Let the best writer cease to produce for a decade and he is as dead as mutton to the critical mind, for no one continues to cherish all the good work he may have done, no one respects the finest outmoded author. Is the mass of production too great now for the critical mind to look back any longer? If that were true, critics would be merely reviewers, but, failing to look back and preserve the past, they fail to create the humus out of which new talents, in order to thrive, must grow. This is a matter that concerns all writers, for the proudest names of our time will vanish with the rest when the fashion of this generation passes away. There is small chance in our fickle air for the hope of a durable fame that has always been thought a legitimate spur of writers. For we throw away our riches like a drunken sailor. As Woodberry lamented long ago in 1881, "Among us literature has no continuous tradition; where the torch fell, it was extinguished." The sorrowful proofs of this are everywhere at hand.

Now the present is "nothing," as C. Day Lewis says, "unless it is spun from a live thread out of the past," and the need of a sense of tradition, or the sense of continuity, has been widely affirmed in recent years. Even James Huneker asserted this when he said it was the one thing lacking to complete the "something powerful" that must emerge from what he described as our "giant amalgam," and Brownell, who said that our heritage was "richer than we realize . . . in all fields," remarked that we "ought to recover our sense" of this. For, as Brownell put it, this should serve as a "binding, cementing force of our civilization." That our writers are generally "handicapped by the lack of a supporting tradition" is the view of a contemporary critic, William Phillips, who adds that "we have not evolved a sense of our national experience that can sustain the modern creative mind." This critic goes on to say that our "avant-garde lacks the sense of nativity" or the "central tradition" that writers in general possess in England and France, the "homogeneous cultural tradition" to which another critic refers and which, as he says, "the writer can take for granted." And why does H. P. Lazarus consider this important? Because it is something "in terms of which" what a writer has to say "will have more than an isolated meaning."

If we lack this sense of a native tradition the reasons are sufficiently obvious now and one of them is that we *are* a "giant amalgam." The influx of new races has destroyed our feeling of continuity, for New England, which produced so many of our classics, seemed remote and unreal to the new immigrant strains that had no natural connection with it. The South and the West, moreover, have been hostile to New England, and this inter-sectional cold war has checked in the general mind any whole-hearted consensus about our tradition. For the rest, with their colonial humility our older critics conveyed no adequate sense of our cultural resources. One might add the further fact that the critic who in our time has done the most to restore the idea of tradition pointedly omitted from his conception of the wholeness of the past the particular foreground of the past that was native to him. As for the sense of a world-tradition, even Walt Whitman defended this, although he had seemed to flout it in his earlier writings. He ceased

to believe that America should break with the past,
as he felt that he himself could never have written
*Leaves of Grass* if he had not stood "bare-headed" before Shakespeare. He wished to think that his work
and America also were what he called the "evolutionary outcome of the past," just as Carl Sandburg,
who had said, "The past is a bucket of ashes," came in
the end to write *Remembrance Rock*. No more than
Whitman would Sandburg repudiate the world-tradition of which the American tradition is an "evolutionary outcome,"—in *Remembrance Rock* he traced,
in point of fact, the origins of the American tradition
in its European setting; but he knew that one can
reach any background only through a foreground and
that, for us, our tradition is the gateway to the rest. It
is our own past, meanwhile, the immediate extension
of the present, that writers need to "support" them,
to "sustain" them, to give their work "more than an
isolated meaning,"—the sense, for one matter, of a
cloud of witnesses who have shared the conditions in
which they live and of what these others have achieved
within their conditions.

That is why, as Eliot said, the writer should have
"in his bones . . . the whole of the literature of his own
country,"—along with "the whole of the literature of
Europe from Homer,"—although Eliot ignored in his
personal canon the whole of American literature and
seemed singularly hostile to its essence. For, saying
that "the culture of each country should be unique,"
he was obliged to reject the uniqueness of this country because it sprang out of ideas which he could

not accept. So we cannot look to Eliot's followers for a sympathetic interest in the literature or the tradition that expresses this uniqueness, though, if these have any value for us, we must defend and cherish them, for to whom else can we look to defend them for us? Can we ask England to do so, even if England maintains in popular editions some of our old writers whom few read at home? I noticed in a recent English review that announced three new studies of Swinburne a reference to Emerson as a once well-known lecturer whose reputation has now quite faded out. But why expect the English to keep Emerson alive for us when they have their own to guard and cherish, so many writers to celebrate with memorial editions, so many writers' birthplaces to mark with plaques? Who doubts the importance of this *in* England, or who doubts in Paris the importance of naming streets after Gautier and Zola, or naming after Littré a telephone-exchange, or picturing Chateaubriand's head on paper money? So on the main street of Dorchester in England one sees statues of William Barnes and Thomas Hardy. What do we do in America that is comparable with this? It took an Englishman, Rudyard Kipling, to be shocked in San Francisco because he found there nothing to commemorate Bret Harte. Nor would he find anything of the kind at present. He would find two memorials to Robert Louis Stevenson, who spent at most a few weeks in the town. But he would still find nothing to remind one of the writer who carried around the world the name of San Francisco.

No one would ever think of asking why the English and the French cherish the great names that express their tradition or why they remembered these great names during the world-movement of the nineteen-twenties that threw "the old cultural furniture" overboard. Everyone recalls the young people asking then, in connection with anything written or composed or painted, whether by Raphael or by Beethoven, by Browning or Brahms, "It may be all right, but what has it got to say to our generation?" If it could not be shown to say something specifically to this generation, out of the window it went, with the codes and the canons which the young were bent on discarding in every country, but this clean sweep was far more complete in America than in England or France because Americans were so largely "cultural tramps" already. This was Ole Rölvaag's phrase for the immigrants who had lost their old European traditions and entered a vacuum in which they were culturally lost because they found no tradition in this country; but the phrase applies equally to many Americans of the older native stocks who were scarcely aware that the country possessed a tradition. For the country was, indeed, as Turgenev said of Russia, *grande et riche, mais désordonnée,* a vast congeries of races and sections that knew so little of this tradition because it had been spread over so large a surface. It had thinned out, moreover, because it was so spread. Owing to this general prevalence of the "cultural tramp" frame of mind, it seemed socially of vital importance to restate this tradition, to make it once more palpable and real, and how much more obviously was this the case when one thought of the writers and artists, who were largely also children of the new immigrant strains. They had become articulate in a world without the centre that many of the older Americans had forgotten, without the sense that one is part of a "great chain of being," a chain that one upholds oneself in turn.

It was to make this clear that I wrote *Makers and Finders,* hoping to connect the literary present with the past, reviving the special kind of memory that fertilizes the living mind and gives it the sense of a base on which to build. I had in my reading discovered traits that many of our writers possessed in common, which gave them a general character that was properly their own, and it struck me that they had contributed to a sort of common fund, a fund of similar experiences, desires and hopes. It seemed to me that, collectively speaking, our writers formed a guild, that they had even worked for a common end,— an elevating end and deeply human—and that living writers, aware of this, could never quite feel as they had felt before, that they were working alone and working in the dark. It was never my intention to attempt to present the "American mind," or to write a literary history in the usual sense, and because of this some of my critics have treated my work as a sort of irresponsible frolic or brainless joy-ride. Reading their reviews, I have felt like Willa Cather's Professor St. Peter when certain other professors reviewed his work, professors who "merely thought he was trying to do the usual thing, and had not succeeded very well."

Whether I had succeeded or not, I was "trying to do something quite different," like Professor St. Peter, trying, among other things, as an integral part of my project, to show the interaction of American letters and life. I had inherited readers who were familiar with Parrington's work,—which I had read in manuscript before it was published,—and who knew the politico-economic phase of our civilization as Veblen and Beard had presented it earlier still. It was therefore no longer my concern to dwell on this phase of the American past, as it was not my concern to dwell on the religious phase that should also have its Parrington in time. So I touched on these phases only lightly with other sides of the social history that Trevelyan has called the "life-blood of civilization." For the rest, my sole criterion was style, which writers must have to rank as writers,—whether they possess "form" or not,—the one indispensable mark of the significant in letters; and I included philosophers, economists and other expository writers along with the poets, historians, novelists and critics when, and only when, they possessed this mark. For then only were they members of the guild with which I was dealing.

Was I too inclusive? When, years ago, planning my history, I told AE about it, he warned me not to write about too many authors,—"Don't take in too many people, only the powers." He added that in American anthologies hundreds of poets were represented who had no right so to appear, "any more than pictures which are not masterpieces have a right to be placed in national galleries." AE was always wise and especially so in this matter at a time when "excernment" seemed to be in order,—Ezra Pound's word for the "weeding out" of what has been performed that the twentieth century mind seemed to require.* Ezra Pound had himself undertaken "reform in reverse of the spirit that disinters," as he said, "forgotten poets," disremembering, so to speak, or causing others to disremember, what was not "basic literature," as he conceived it. Expressing the spirit of an age that felt it necessary to throw over much of the cargo to save the ship, he drew up a selective canon that paralleled in its way President Eliot's popular "five-foot shelf." For this there appeared to be reasons enough, among them the mass of new knowledge which the widening of the human horizon enjoined on readers, as the tendency to internationalism confronted the national mind with traditions that were alien to its own tribal past. If one had to know more of Arabia and Persia or the writers of India and China, one had to forget the lesser in one's own tradition, beginning with the vast expanse of writing in which people pretended to be at home but for which, with time, they had lost all genuine feeling. One had obviously to ask the question, in thinking of the past, how much should one endeavor to keep alive, how much of one's own national past at

---

* "You cannot get the whole cargo of a sinking paedeuma onto the lifeboat. If you propose to have any live literature of the past kept in circulation . . . there has got to be more attention to the best and the basic."—Ezra Pound, *Polite Essays.*

a time when every literature has to compete with world-literature for its place in the sun.

In short, I could not ignore the wisdom of AE's advice or of Ezra Pound's practice of excernment, although the theory of this was far from valid. For Pound spoke of excernment as the "ordering of knowledge so that the next man (or generation) can most readily find the live part of it and waste the least possible time among obsolete issues," while, in fact, to the next generation, the "live part" of the literary past will be totally different from the part that is live for Pound. Then he and the issues he stands for will be obsolete also, and the next generation will require a part of the past that accords with its own tastes and prepossessions. Every generation makes its own choice of the past, and no man's private canon can anticipate this, though Pound spoke nevertheless for a day that is nothing if not selective, whether its selection will appeal to the future or not. In reaction against commercialism, in distrust of "numbers," the critical mind was never more exclusive, given as it is to admitting the merit of a few chosen writers alone and ignoring the multiplicity of other talents. To write the twenty-fifth book on Melville or the twenty-eighth on Henry James, or one more essay on John Donne or Yeats, seems to this critical mind of more importance than to write the first book on James Huneker or Ernest Fenollosa. The critics in question presuppose that they are concerned with the "best" when this best may be only the best for their own decade, and when perhaps they have nothing to say that is new concerning this and might make some real contribution on a less fashionable level. But, however that may be, I knew that to "take in too many people" was not merely to disregard AE's injunction. It was also to court the hostility of critics who have largely followed Pound and who have almost established a tradition of their own.

That the major and the minor should never be confused is surely one of the laws of criticism, and any overvaluation one sets on the minor detracts from the appreciation of the transcendent. "The laudation of the unworthy," as Poe said, "is to the worthy the most bitter of all wrongs," though this is not the same thing as discussing the "unworthy" or including minor figures in historical studies. How many of these did not Poe discuss, and even belaud, in his critical essays, and how many did not Dr. Johnson include in his *Lives of the Poets,* from Yalden, Garth, Hammond and Fenton to Christopher Pitt? Did not his life of Richard Savage exceed in space, besides, his treatment of Congreve, Gay, Addison or Swift?—facts that, so great is the eminence of Johnson, dignify the question of the relation between history and the minor writer. Leo Stein, an acute critic, praised Arber's *New Anthology* because "by giving so many minor men" it supplied "a sort of atmosphere to the people one knows," and how sympathetically T. S. Eliot refers to Charles Whibley's discussion of the minor authors and journalists of the past in England. Whibley, says Eliot, did not talk about these writers "to elevate them above their proper place" but because "we can touch the life of the great works of literature of any age all the better if we know something of the less." In somewhat the same spirit, Lafcadio Hearn, in one of his letters, dwelt on the mistake of "keeping to the masterpieces only,"—another observer who justified me in failing to follow AE's advice and reversing Pound's procedure of excernment. I might add here that the masterpieces of one generation have often been the minor works of a previous age, as John Donne, a master of our moment, seemed minor in the past and will undoubtedly seem so again in the future. For "metaphysics" will become once more, as it formerly was, a term of abuse, and Donne will return again to the admired obscurity from which the twentieth century rescued him. Only a handful of writers are perennially "great," and every generation selects its own affinities in the past, the writers who are congenial to its own special nature. For the rest, I had other reasons for including minor writers,—whom I feel reasonably sure I have not overvalued,—reasons that sprang for me out of my subject. I was concerned to illustrate the truth of a statement, in the London *Times Literary Supplement,* by an anonymous writer, that, besides "continuity," what "bodies out a culture" is the "circumfusing variegated bulk of lesser genius." This was the point that, years before, I had noted in André Gide's remark, "It suddenly seemed clear to me that if there were no names in the history of art except those belonging to the creators of new forms there would be no culture. The very word implies a continuity, and therefore it calls for disciples, imitators and followers to make a living chain; in other words, a tradition."

It was just this "living chain,"—Byron's "electric chain" or, one might say, the "magnetic chain" of Hawthorne,—the chain that somehow communicates life to everyone who has it in his hand that I wished, in American terms, to create a sense of. Would not this give existing writers a feeling that they were sustained by colleagues and partners among their antecedents, while the mass of these alone might convey a consciousness of the richness and the weight of our tradition? Was not the famous "loneliness" of the American writer due in part to the general ignorance of the great number of American writers, mostly the "disciples" and "imitators" of whom Gide speaks? One might call these the coral insects who add their single cells to the great structure of the republic of letters, the literary rank and file who had made possible, Goethe said, his own good fortune, his advent, his influence, his career.

In this country, for the rest, unless one has the whole account, can one know which is the greater and which is the less, considering that Melville and Emily Dickinson were regarded as minor for many years when they were not ignored altogether? Was not Henry Adams ignored during his lifetime, and was not Henry Osborn Taylor right when he observed that this "throws a sort of faint sidelight on the culture of his country?" And what shall one say of the ignoring of Henry Osborn Taylor? Or of Henry Charles Lea, scarcely mentioned in literary histories, although his own *History of the Inquisition* would have been one of the national glories if this great historian had lived in England or France? In this matter are the modish critics of our day, with their party line, more to be trusted than the critics of fifty years ago? That they are aesthetically keener nobody questions, but, in regard to essential values, they are more at sea than the critics who were bred in the old humane tradition. For fashion is no longer obliged to submit to tradition, the sum of all the fashions of the past, which kept each fashion within bounds by measuring it against the rest,—another reason for reviving the sense of tradition. There is no force today to keep fashion in its place, and fashion condemns as promiscuous whatever transgresses its small decrees and follows its own independent curiosity instead. It condemns unread whatever it has not discovered, and what has it discovered itself in the writing of the past?—the past of a country in which, for all that fashion knows, there may be other "unknown" Melvilles for other generations. While this may be unlikely, fashion cannot say so until all the buried reputations have been exhumed, as the reputations of Ambrose Bierce and John Lloyd Stephens have been exhumed, with those of Emily Dickinson and Henry Adams. And sometimes these have to be not only exhumed but reconstructed, as a paleontologist reconstructs a dinosaur from a handful of bones. Until quite recently American literature was a No Man's Land, in which an explorer was obliged to follow every clue, for it had never been properly mapped and one had to know the whole of it before one could rightly forget any of its parts. Where so many talents were buried and lost, one was obliged to "disinter," instead of "excerning," in the manner of Ezra Pound, for no cumulative memory existed in this land whose motto was "out of nowhere into nothing."

Perhaps I had felt this more keenly than one could feel it in our day because of the Cimmerian darkness that surrounded my youth,—that is to say, regarding the question of who was who and what was what in the world of American ideas and American talent. In those days writers like Henry B. Fuller and Thorstein Veblen were ignored or obscure while blatant mediocrities filled the literary foreground, and I did not know that in England and France one found similar incomprehensions, sporadically, of course, in a lesser degree. Did not Browning astonish a friend in London by saying he had just seen George Borrow, whom everyone supposed had been dead for thirty years? And did not Doughty of *Arabia Deserta* ask, "who is Thomas Hardy?" when both were octogenarians and virtually neighbors? Did not Fragonard, the painter, die in Paris as obscurely as any artist ever died in New York, unhonored by even the single line of obituary vouchsafed to Greuze, although both had symbolized epochs in the art of France? Both died equally penniless and equally forgotten. One could tell hundreds of similar stories of a kind that my own generation naively regarded as typical of our unawakened country, although this does not alter the fact that we have been singularly unaware of our talents and intellectual resources. And how ignorant of our history too, not our political history but the kind of social and cultural history that critics are obliged to know if they are to deal adequately with talents of the past or the present. And are not novelists obliged to know this also if they are to present three-dimensional characters and scenes? When Dreiser speaks of farmhouses in Wyoming in 1828 he shakes the reader's confidence in his knowledge of the West, or all of the West his eyes had not actually seen, just as one questioned the authenticity of Weir Mitchell's picture of the Revolutionary time when he spoke of the miniaturist Malbone as an English painter. When Mencken, followed by Ezra Pound, said that FitzGerald's Omar Khayyám was "our first introduction" to Oriental culture, he ignored one of the major facts in the history of American culture, the Persian and Hindu studies of Emerson and Thoreau. Regarded individually, these misconceptions are slight enough, but regarded collectively, with hundreds of others that any historian must bring to light, they invalidate countless generalizations of American critics. How many, for instance, have said over and over that the generation of the nineteen-twenties was the first "younger generation" in American letters, whereas three previous generations had not only used the phrase but had been fully and equally entitled to use it. And what shall one say of the unpublished books of which one catches glimpses in memoirs and letters that have appeared in print,—manuscripts naturally forgotten in a country in which no one has had the enterprise even to reëdit George Ticknor's journal of

travel.* Yet is this not surely one of the most enter-
taining pictures of the Europe of Byron and Goethe
that has ever appeared? What great themes, moreover,
lie undiscovered in the cultural past of the United
States, the story of the diaspora, for instance, of the
Southerners after the Civil War who drifted to London, to Mexico, to Honduras, to Egypt. And what a
tale is that of the New England missionaries who
translated the Bible into a score of tongues, who established the first printing-presses in Bulgaria and Malta
and conducted the only school in Athens in 1825. How
many leaders in how many countries were educated in
the schools which they founded all over Polynesia and
all over Asia. Our history is almost as full of surprises
and wonders as the China that Marco Polo saw.

When some of my critics ask ironically why I mention this writer or that,—the author of Thayer's *Beethoven,* for instance, or Charles Godfrey Leland,—I
wonder if it ever occurs to them that I am not promis-

---

* What, for instance, has become of the manuscript journal
of the "first American archæologist," as Charles Eliot Norton
called him,—John Izard Middleton of South Carolina, who
served Mme. de Staël as a model for Lord Nevil in *Corinne?*
The journal, supposedly preserved in Baltimore, contains his
recollections not only of his visits to Mme. de Staël at Coppet
in 1806-1807 but of Mme. Récamier also.

What has become of the two volumes of memoirs,—"for personal reasons" never printed,—of Madame Le Vert, the famous
great lady of Mobile?

What has become of Paul Hamilton Hayne's life of William
Gilmore Simms,—the unpublished biography of the most important writer of the old South by the second most important
writer? Or of Simms's unpublished edition of *Mother Goose,*
which would surely be a literary curiosity if there ever was one?

cuous but that they are ignorant, culpably, themselves. Not that Leland was very important, but that, in following the gypsies, he stood for a strain of wildness in the American mind, and, besides, one has reasons for thinking that certain of these lesser men will interest the future more than they interest the present. I may add that in writing of others I had no thought of reviving them,—I wrote because they *cannot* be revived and yet because they should be known, or known about, at least, inasmuch as they convey the feeling of their place and their time. There are many irreclaimable novelists and novels,—most of John W. De Forest and all of Edgar Fawcett, for another example,—that are good for one purpose only, but very good for that, to have social history as it were distilled from them. I have used numbers of these myself to re-create the atmosphere in which the greater writers arose and flourished, for they were often shrewd observers of their time. I wished, for the rest, to trace the interrelations between the various writers and their various worlds, interlocked as the writers have been, following and influencing one another, as no historian had adequately shown before. I had been surprised to find how densely integrated the literary experience and tradition of Americans had been, how closely linked the writers were and even the regions in a literary way, how independent of the writers of any other country. It struck me that no one had realized to what a degree our literature had been self-perpetuating and self-sustaining, after, one might say, 1840, and this explained the constant cross-references to which I resorted throughout my books, wishing to create a sense of these intricate relations. To do so seemed all the more needful because, in so many biographies, in the want of this sense, the subject has hung in a void. Since I have spoken of Henry Charles Lea, may I note that in the only life of him one finds no mention of Henry Adams or Henry Osborn Taylor, the rival contemporary students of the mediæval mind, nor is there anything to suggest that Lea was one of a long line of American scholars, including Irving, Ticknor and Prescott, who were concerned with Spain. Similarly, books have been written on Bierce with scarcely any reference to the other California writers with whom he was connected, or any visible knowledge of the novels by Charles Warren Stoddard and Josiah Royce in which these authors appeared as characters. Even in the little field of the Norwegian-American writers biographies have been written of both Rölvaag and Veblen in neither of which was the other mentioned, although they were contemporaries and throw light on one another. And how odd it is that anyone could write of Rölvaag and his pioneers without associating these with Hamlin Garland's or with Willa Cather's pioneers in the further West, considering how mutually illuminating all of them are. How much more valuable, how much richer these biographies would have been if their subjects were related to the contexts that are proper to them.

So much for the use and importance of a sense of the tradition that "assures the continuity of creation," as Stravinsky puts it, important especially in the

United States where there are probably more writers today than there were on the whole face of the planet two hundred years ago. And is it not also important to possess the sense of community here, along with the sense of continuity?—and for this one must see literature in relation to the society from which its springs, although in criticism this is not now the fashion. It is true, no doubt, that first-rate works have an existence of their own that is virtually independent of their place and time, but this is not true of the secondary works that largely make up a tradition, as one sees, for example, in considering our literature of the South. How could one understand the antebellum Southern writers if one knew nothing of the "Cotton Kingdom" which they were bent on glorifying, or the postwar generation of romancers that so sorrowfully regretted the passing of this old regime? Similarly, the whole point of Ellen Glasgow's work was that it restored the feeling of reality and truth, again in terms of the Southern social scene; and something of this kind might be said of the literature of all the American regions as well as of the nation itself, generally speaking. Moreover, in dealing with writers of the past, one must sympathize with their state of mind, one must accept them, in part, on their own terms, adopting Coleridge's "willing suspension of disbelief" in the values that meant so much to them.* For how

* "To appreciate the art of another period one must, to a certain extent, enter into its spirit, accept its conventions, adopt a 'willing suspension of disbelief' in its values. For if we have no sympathy for what it is trying to say, we shall not be able

can one properly judge them if one fails to do so? If my own *The World of Washington Irving* was in tone buoyantly optimistic, it was because I felt this to be true: I shared, for many months when I wrote the book, the infectious springtime feeling of the young republic. And why was there so much "landscape" in my New England volumes? Because I was living for a while with the writers of a rural age for whom the realities of the countryside were vitally important. I saw Longfellow as his contemporaries saw this poet, as even Baudelaire must have seen him or he would not have written *Le Calumet de Paix* or borrowed from Longfellow twice in *Les Fleurs du Mal*. But was I seriously "nostalgic" for Longfellow's time? This word has been applied to my writing so often that I feel compelled to meet the charge, and I may say that it is true if I can be called nostalgic also for the twenty-first century and the ages of Pericles and Homer. I am nostalgic for every epoch and decade of history when I have once caught the feeling of it. But this is a quality of imagination, simply, and it has none of the overtones of sickness which the world nostalgia usually connotes. I have enjoyed Theodore Dreiser more than Longfellow, and my imagination has since been equally at home with the writers of the Western prairies and the East Side of New York.

May I say one further word about the method that I have pursued and that may well suggest the method of a novel, introducing and reintroducing the char-

to judge if it says it well."—Lord David Cecil, *Early Victorian Novelists*.

acters and scenes, while every phrase I have used is founded on fact. If I mingled the novelists and the poets together it was because the literary genres were not, in my scheme, very important, and a novelist and a poet of the same milieu seemed to me to have more in common than two poets or two novelists of different times and places. Similarly, I wove in historians and critics, not always classified as such, belonging to the climate of their time or creators of it, for is not a writer who creates a climate as creative in the true sense as one who creates fictional characters or literary forms? Was Veblen less creative than Edith Wharton? I have ignored, in short, the conventional distinction between De Quincey's "literature of power" and "literature of knowledge," so long as both are literature, properly speaking, ignoring too the commonplace of our day that Ambrose Bierce expressed in one of his letters: "Literature,—a word which I beg him to observe means fiction." Literature has never been synonymous with fiction in any of the great ages. Replying further to the charge that I express no judgments, may I say that the reader will find my writers *judged*, though the judgments are often presented indirectly in the proportions of the work or conveyed by modulations of style and tone. As for what many may regard as my excessive amplitude, I have courted there again the hostility of critics at a time which Paul Valéry described as a time not for long works but for sudden perceptions, for fragments, for the *précis* and the sketch.

But all these personal matters are trivial beside the

great question of the use of tradition, which establishes a consensus about the dead and which causes them to live again, to fructify the present, to fertilize existing minds, and to stabilize our values. Unless they are related to a sense of the past, no statements regarding the present, moreover, can ever be found to wear well in the future or to express the kind of mature self-knowledge and self-respect that any literature must have to count greatly in the world.

# CHAPTER III

## BEYOND ADOLESCENCE

Is THE LITERATURE of this country ripe for the world position that has been thrust upon it, largely because of the exhaustion of the European peoples? No one questions the immense vitality, the fertility, the force of the American mind in literature as in other departments of life, but is it not still, on the whole, confused and as far from equal to this world role as the foreign policy of the nation has proved to be? Does not our literature reflect, just like our foreign policy, a national mind that has not yet crystallized, that has not reached an equipoise and cannot put forth its full strength but remains, with its intelligence and buoyancy, still immature? Gertrude Stein, an astute observer, said of the American soldiers who appeared in France in 1945 that a great change had come over them since the first world war, for they had lost their provinciality, they were sure of themselves as they listened and talked, accustomed to many human types and ways of living. A somewhat similar change perhaps has come over American writers,—the great new twentieth-century citizen army that is no less marked in literature than it is in the field,—but are they not rather collectively than individually more mature, though the nation has been rapidly and obviously coming of age?

It has often been said that our literature is a literature of boys. Many of our classics have survived as classics for boys, or one might better say that Cooper, Irving, Longfellow, Dana, the author of *Two Years Before the Mast,* have largely survived as classics for adolescents. T. S. Eliot has plausibly found a lack of the maturity in Poe that "comes only with the maturing of the man as a whole," and certain it is that, like Mark Twain in quite another way, Poe is preëminently a writer for adolescents. Was there not something of the boy-philosopher in William James, moreover, the philosopher who was once asked to be "serious for a moment"?—and is this not even one of James's charms?—while many writers of more recent years have suggested overgrown exuberant boys, John Reed, for one, the "playboy of the Russian revolution." Jack London played outlaw and pirate to the end of his life, and Sherwood Anderson's adolescent gropings were matched by those of Thomas Wolfe, a writer of genius who never quite grew up. Then there was Vachel Lindsay, adolescent from first to last, and Mencken, who has so often suggested "Peck's Bad Boy." What has been said of our civilization, that it was always beginning again, at the same level, on each new frontier, might perhaps be said of our literature also. It is always beginning again as adolescent.

True, or half true, as this is, there might be nothing regrettable in it if writers, remaining "young," remained buoyant and vital, as E. E. Cummings remains buoyant and vital, the poet who has retained for thirty years the freshness, the gaiety, the wonder, the curiosity of youth. For the rest, the youthfulness of the American mind, its adventurousness and zest, has been the great gift of America to the older countries, and one might ask why America should not remain adolescent,—is not a high-spirited boy better than a tired old man? But, good as the traits of youth may be, it is not good to be immature when this means the arrested development that is common with our writers, when "incompleteness" and "truncation," as Irving Howe says, have been "so pervasive" in our culture. Mr. Howe, writing on Sherwood Anderson, observes, as many have observed before, that "the early achievement of American writers" is "seldom enlarged in maturity," while he dwells on the "bewilderment" and the "disappointment" of Anderson himself when Thomas Wolfe brutally told him that he was "finished." This has been for thirty years almost a commonplace of American critics, who have said that, with us, the abortive career is the rule, that something "happens" to American writers, that their talents fizzle out, that "there are no second acts in American lives." How many writers have realized themselves that they were "prematurely cracked, like an old plate," as Scott Fitzgerald put it? As the young writer says in Saroyan's *The Assyrian and Other Stories*, "Exuberance did the trick, but now it doesn't . . . It did the trick for Thomas Wolfe, as long as he lived, and for a lot of others too, but exuberance seems to stop when a man gets past his middle thirties, or the man himself stops." Saroyan is saying of the American writer what Mrs. Lightfoot Lee said in Henry Adams's novel long ago, "You grow six inches high and then you stop. Why will not somebody grow to be a tree and cast a shadow?" In *Green Hills of Africa,* Hemingway said much the same thing: "Something happens to our good writers at a certain age." Hemingway added, "We do not have great writers . . . We destroy them in certain ways."

But is it true that "we" destroy them? Is not this a fallacy which has also become a commonplace of American critics? I cannot feel as I used to feel when I wrote *The Ordeal of Mark Twain* that writers fail because of external conditions, because "we" or their wives and their friends destroy them, or editors, or publishers, or the pressure of the world they live in, or public opinion. It is largely an illusion that writers "fall" to Hollywood or Broadway as women who stooped to folly were once said to fall; for is this not often, at least, with writers, a question rather of finding their natural level? And this may be a progress up as well as down, since writing may exist that is worse than "popular" writing. For, after all, popular writing amuses a good many people, while abortive "serious" writing has no value whatever. As for the popular writers themselves, they practise their art in perfect good faith and seldom feel that they have "fallen" to it, for they have a talent of their own that others can acquire only by strenuous effort, the opposite of falling. "It is known to comparatively few that the production of successful pot-boilers is an art in itself," as Edith Wharton said,—referring to the "heroic abstentions" of a character of hers that were not "purely voluntary," as she put it,—though "the artist who would rather starve than paint a pot-boiler" remains "a favourite figure of imaginative youth." No, serious writers seldom fall, at least in any significant sense, nor can it be said properly that "we" destroy them, although without doubt they *are* destroyed because they are thwarted as writers, even to the point where they lose the will to live. That there is a talent which is "death to hide," which, hidden, or balked, or undeveloped, brings on death, innumerable writers have shown in America, as elsewhere. Was not Jack London's suicide plainly a result of this frustration, like Vachel Lindsay's suicide, like Hart Crane's later? —as, ordered to stop drinking, Scott Fitzgerald drank all the more, said one of his friends, because he did not "wish to get well."

But what are we asking for? Do we Americans expect too much when "normally," as Sainte-Beuve remarked, "fifteen years constitute a literary career"? Is it not known that under the best conditions many writers are nervously exhausted in the middle of their lives? Have not defeat, disease, disappointment and early death characterized the lives of writers in all times and countries? The literary temperament is prone to the stresses and strains that have made the "calamities of authors" everywhere a byword; and yet the complaints of so many Americans can scarcely be ignored, nor can the evidence of so many American lives. That American talent fails to mature in countless cases we all know, and, if this is not because "we" destroy it, what can be the reason unless that the talent is destroyed by the writers themselves? That this is the case, in fact, Hemingway says in another of his stories, referring to the young writer in *The Snows of Kilimanjaro,* "He had destroyed his talent himself. Why should he blame this woman because she kept him well? He had destroyed his talent by not using it, by betrayals of himself and what he believed in, by drinking so much that he blunted the edge of his perceptions, by laziness, by sloth and by snobbery, by pride and by prejudice, by hook and by crook. It was a talent all right but instead of using it he had traded on it." There are surely plenty of reasons here to explain the "truncation" of American talents in this or that or the other of a hundred cases, and they all boil down to a generalization of another remark of Scott Fitzgerald's, "I had been only a mediocre caretaker of my talent." True or not in Fitzgerald's case, this is surely true in scores of others, and inevitably it leads one to the question, What is a *good* caretaker of one's talent? The biblical parable of the talents, referring to money, is equally germane in this other connection, the psychological problem of the writer's life.

This is one of the weightier matters that critics have ignored in their recent preoccupation with the mint and cummin, the grammatical and rhetorical minutiae of literary texts, concerned as they are with form alone, with "the letter that giveth life,"—T. S. Eliot's reversal of the words of the gospel. For have not the new critics devoted to craftsmanship so much zeal that they have had none to spare for other questions? How many writers' conferences, how many summer schools, how many classes, how many books and magazines dwell each year, with fanatical concentration, on the "form" of writing, never diverting a moment's thought from the question, How to write well, to the question, How to live well to be a writer? Who ever speaks of the kind of life that writers should lead to become great writers or the way to use their energy to develop their powers? Who considers what taking good care of one's talent means? Who thinks of maturity as desirable or worthy of study? The cult of youth that has dominated writers since even before the first world war, from Edna Millay to Hemingway and Fitzgerald, has filled them with a fear of growing old that almost precludes at the outset any regard for the uses of growing up. Concerned with literary technique alone, oblivious of what might be called the more important technique of literary living, they are apt to end with the feeling of Fitzgerald in *The Crack-up,*—the "feeling that I was standing at twilight on a deserted range, with an empty rifle in my hands and the targets down."

Now in this connection I have referred to Scott Fitzgerald so many times that I must add a further word about him. How far can one say that he failed as a writer when he dramatized his failure and expressed his predicament in such fine images and phrases? Certainly Fitzgerald made more of his life than all but a handful in his time, so that he has left behind a brilliant legend, though one feels that he retained the point of view of the spellbound boy who could say "The very rich are different from us." One has only to compare Turgenev's *Smoke* with Fitzgerald's *Tender is the Night*,—and these two novels are comparable in many respects,—to see how Turgenev took "the very rich" in his stride and judged them from the mature man's point of view. He cleared the decks at once of any "romantic awe" of the rich,— Hemingway's phrase for Fitzgerald,—and got down to the basic realities at the very outset, whereas Fitzgerald never cleared the decks, for the dazzling outside was enough for him.* It was nothing to Turgenev that his people had *savoir faire,* along with the "repose" that Fitzgerald valued so highly, and, taking all this for granted, he was able to judge them in the light of essential human values. But for Fitzgerald

---

* Turgenev's *Smoke* dealt with the Russian "smart set" in exile in a European watering-place, as Fitzgerald dealt with smart Americans in Europe, and Turgenev's judgment of them might have applied equally well to Fitzgerald's Riviera circle: "What stale trash, what worthless trifles, what barren futilities occupied all those hearts and minds . . . at all days and hours, throughout the breadth and depth of their existence! . . . And, at bottom, what ignorance! What lack of understanding of all that human life is built upon and of all that adorns it!"

What provides the scale in *Smoke* is the mind of young Litvinov, through whose eyes we see these generals and countesses. It is Litvinov who speaks for the author and whose "thoughts were very far away and moved in a world that was very different from his present surroundings." Fitzgerald was never able to see his wasters in this mature perspective. He felt that his doctor, Dick Diver, had become a "gigolo" and in some sense had therefore failed, but he conveyed no conception of the "very different" world that, *if he had not failed,* Diver *would have stood for.*

these *were* the dominant values, like the "fabulous style" in which his people travelled, with their servants, their dogs, their trappings and their luggage; so he had no standard by which to affirm that wishing to "have a good time," the sole life-aim of his people, was adolescent. Fitzgerald remained the college boy who could refer, in a story, to "a fading but still lovely woman of twenty-seven," and what he felt as the betrayal of his gift was undoubtedly a sense that, for some reason, he had not grown up.* One might ask, moreover, if Hemingway has grown up either, notwithstanding his great story *The Old Man and the Sea*. Has he not remained the swaggering boy who suggested Mike Fink to Gertrude Stein and who feels that he has "knocked" Turgenev "out of the ring"?

But what is growing up? What does growth mean with a man who is a writer? Is this not a question of the art of literary living? When I was the literary editor of *The Freeman,* thirty years ago, there was a French writer, Jules Bois, living in New York, who

* Regarding Scott Fitzgerald, a friend in England writes to me: "In those stories of the 1920's it is all of a piece. Not one of these fellows makes any mention of the purpose of college or of higher education or any obligation connected therewith. Although there may be references to reciting or discussing poetry, there are never any to study or knowledge or intellectual activity. Always girls; and when a youth meets with any kind of slight or disappointment, he has only one choice,—either to get blind drunk or resort to a prostitute.

"What a juvenile and how tragic a mess he made of things! . . . Are we to infer that this life and misery are part of the destiny of the writer in America? . . . Graham Wallas used to ask in the 1920's: Why not a group movement among the young intellectuals inspired by sobriety, hard work and cheerfulness?"

used to come into my office to discuss a book he proposed to write and publish perhaps as a serial in our weekly paper. After writing about Mark Twain myself, I was full of the question of the American writer and why so many talents fizzled out here, why so many American careers seemed to be abortive and why American writers lived so blindly. It was obvious to me that Jules Bois' project would throw some light on this, for he intended to show what a fully developed career might be and what steps a writer might take in order to achieve it. His subject and his title were suggested by *The Imitation of Christ,* which he always carried about in his pocket with him, and Jules Bois hoped to parallel this *vade mecum* of the Christian life with a manual of the literary life for the guidance of writers. In planning *The Imitation of Goethe* he felt that this greatest of Germans had known, and possibly better than anyone else, how a writer can best coin the metal that is in him, how he should live in order to make the best use of all his powers, how meet, for this purpose, the various contingencies of life. Where should a writer live, what people should he choose to know, how should he travel, how read, how divide his hours, how regulate his habits, his appetites, his interests, his passions? While Jules Bois was well aware that writers can scarcely be classified, that they are more individualized than other types, he knew they had certain characteristics and needs in common, and, aware as well of the powerful role that emulation plays in life, he felt that Goethe might serve them in a way as a model.

That book Jules Bois never wrote, but when, along with all the world, I discovered Albert Schweitzer, I found that in a sense this great man had written it for him. For Schweitzer related how he had imitated Goethe, finding in him a model on many occasions. Having doubts himself about studying medicine, he had seen how Goethe allowed Wilhelm Meister to become a surgeon and how Goethe too, for peremptory reasons, abandoned other work to return to the natural sciences at a certain moment. Schweitzer, obliged to labour at accounts when his mind was full of other plans, was able to remember Goethe spending hours straightening out the finances of a small German state; while, as a young man, he had been struck by Goethe's account in the *Harzreise* of a journey he had made through November mist and rain. Goethe had visited with "suitable help" a minister's son who was in "spiritual difficulties," and thereafter, when Schweitzer had to undertake some irksome task, he would say to himself, "There is a Harzreise for you." He had found Goethe haunted by anxiety about justice, and, reduced himself to despair in Africa, he could think of Goethe's last plan for Faust, to win back land from the sea on which men might live. Then, remembering the vigorous eager way in which Goethe shared the life of his age in its thought and its activity alike, Schweitzer felt standing beside him in the forest this "man who really understood" and who had so often been his model.

It is true enough that Schweitzer is a writer of a special type, apparently as remote as possible from

Scott Fitzgerald, but, if not a great writer, he is a great man writing, and humanly mature, as Goethe was. Goethe's life, besides, had other aspects in which other types can find their own tendencies corroborated and, if need be, corrected, and he has in fact served as a model for many writers. For is not the instinct of emulation one of the strongest in imaginative minds and perhaps the most powerful force in a writer's education? Everyone remembers how, as a boy, Alexander Pope dreamed of seeing Dryden whom at last he saw and whom he regarded as poetry in a bodily form, as Dostoievsky's first act on visiting Petersburg, still a boy, was to seek out Pushkin's old chambers and the site of his duel. Dostoievsky would have put on mourning at the news of Pushkin's death if he had not been wearing it already for his mother, expressing the mood of hero-worship that writers naturally feel in their youth and that springs from their need of models to shape their careers. Our age has had small faith in heroes because it has seen so many false heroes, the Hitlers and Mussolinis who have been tribal idols, and it inherits, moreover, the mood of the "debunkers." But has not William Carlos Williams said that the "example" of Henri Fabre has "always stood beside" him "as a measure and a rule"? "It has made me quiet," Williams says, "and induced in me a patient industry and . . . a long-range contentment"; and was it not partly Fabre's example that "behooved" him to "be at one's superlative best" and to "work single-mindedly for the task"? That hero-worship still exists, although it is not recognized and operates behind a screen, as one might say, one can see in the deep South where Faulkner's example and presence have given birth to a whole school of writers. For we must have models in our minds to discipline ourselves, images of the kind of perfection we wish to attain, and writers have always attested that these models are necessary to serve them as pace-makers and criteria for their development and growth. The only question for a given writer is to have the models that are best *for him,* that will forward his own particular development and growth.

If American writers fail to develop, if, so often, they fail to grow, is not this therefore a question that one ought to examine? Have these writers lacked models, or have they followed the wrong models, and in any case what is the reason for it? When, speaking of William James, whom he did not consider a true philosopher, Santayana suggested that, in his youth, James had never seen a philosopher "whom he would have cared to resemble," this writer was rash perhaps on two accounts. For, in the first place, James was undoubtedly a true philosopher, and moreover he had seen Emerson, whom he admired immensely. But how right is this point of Santayana's in other connections. How many living American writers have grown up in a world that afforded no hint of a model for their emulation, so that in their youth they never saw a writer whom they would have "cared to resemble" and scarcely heard of one in their country or their region? And was it not natural that, driven abroad for their models, they should sometimes have followed models who were not good *for them?*

But what is a "good" model? Does one mean a good man in the sense of the old Chinese painter, "If one's moral character is not high, one's art will correspondingly lack style"? Milton corroborated this when he said that a writer "ought himself to be a true poem" if he "wishes to write well . . . in laudable things"; and of what was Gauguin thinking when he said, "With the masters I converse. Their example fortifies me. When I am tempted to falter I blush before them"? Was he not referring to personal nobility also, or at least to the "conscience" and "patience" that Rodin described as the two fundamental traits of the life of an artist? But if this were taken to mean that the writer must be a good man in the ordinary sense, that his nature must be harmonious, it would be far too simple, for there must be, as AE said, all manner of contraries in a writer's nature to intensify the interaction of his faculties and parts. I remember an eminent English critic saying to me once, "Have you noticed that the best men are sometimes the worst writers and that sometimes the best writers are the worst men?" I had noticed this indeed, though it never made me happy, as it seems to make those who believe in "salvation by sin." How often one is obliged to notice it! Was not Cicero, unquestionably great as a writer, in his personal nature a double-dealer, treacherous, unscrupulous, a braggart, a coward and a liar, as his latest editor proves from the evidence of his letters, and in how many writers has one found the kind of disruption and conflict out of which have sprung great works of the imagination? For there must be darkness in literature as well as light, descents into hell as well as paradises, a fact we are not likely to forget at a time when Rimbaud and Baudelaire have played so large a part in the minds of writers. At this time when life itself has seemed the "dark dream" of which Rimbaud wrote, it is natural that these two poets have been so magnetic and that Rimbaud has been the idol of literary youth all over the world, the voice of its impatience with the past and its impulse of destruction. He was a great virtuoso at a moment when virtuosity seemed more important than ever to the literary mind, one of the word-revolutionists whose verbal and technical innovations outrivalled those of Pound later and possibly Joyce. He too had descended into hell like millions in a war-sick world, like thousands of sensitive minds who shared his disillusion with the standards of a civilization that was wrecking the world and who found in him both a prophet and a brother, another "man who really understood."

Thus Rimbaud became a model for the twentieth-century literary mind as Goethe had been universally a century before, and for much the same reason, odd as it seems, because the main object of both these poets had been to develop their faculties to the highest degree. For to become a seer was Rimbaud's aim in all he did, and this had been the aim of Goethe also, while the intensity with which both pursued it explained their power over other minds, irrespective of all the immeasurable differences between them.

Both had followed models before they were models themselves in turn, and Rimbaud's special model was Baudelaire, who had said it was through dreaming that man entered into communication with the rich dark world that surrounds him. It was to see in this dark world that Rimbaud used all known means to induce in himself the state of perpetual dreaming, and he supposed he was following his master in depraving himself deliberately by what he called the "derangement of all the senses." He believed that one could not become a seer without transcending the old conceptions of humanity, of good and evil, and in order to make his work as an artist his sole and only virtue he consciously sought what he called "monstrosity of soul." But this was not only remote from Goethe's conception of becoming a seer, it was equally remote from Baudelaire's, for Rimbaud had never seen the letters in which, by implication, Baudelaire passionately repudiated just this notion. Far from approving of what, to him, were weaknesses and vices, he described his horrified struggles to cast them off, regarding the taking of drugs, which he tried, as no less immoral than suicide, and rejecting the "artificial paradises" to which they led. Not to be willing to accept what he described as the conditions of life was to betray one's soul, Baudelaire said, and he would have been the first to add that, as a model, Rimbaud was good only for the "devil's party." For he did not wish to belong to this party himself.

There are excellent authorities for those who feel that one *should go* to the devil if one's deepest convictions and impulses lead that way, and Rimbaud possessed, as a writer, the "conscience" and even the "patience," perhaps, that made him a good model from Rodin's point of view. But, in this connection, a further question arises, What is the nature of the disciple who follows the model? For, in any given case, a model must be *congruous* before it can be described as a good model, one that is not discordant with one's own personal aptitudes, one's mental conformation and essential aims. This is the question that involves so many American writers and the models they have followed mistakenly so many times, as it seems obvious that, for one, Hart Crane was mistaken in following Rimbaud when he wished to write a great poem in the tradition of Walt Whitman. Yvor Winters, writing on Crane, suggests that he followed the model, or followed at least the counsel, of Whitman himself, saying that the doctrines of Whitman, and Emerson, if really put into practice, would naturally lead a man to suicide. What we appear to have, says Winters, is "a poet of great genius who ruined his life and his talent by living and writing as the two greatest religious leaders of our nation recommend," for did they not say that men should cultivate all their impulses, and what, in the end, could be more suicidal than this? But when one thinks of Emerson, with all his checks and balances, and of Whitman's "clear sun shining" and "fresh air blowing," one feels compelled to look for another explanation,—for whoever committed suicide by following these?—and was not Rimbaud "constantly" in Hart Crane's mind during the months when, as Philip Horton says, he was planning *The Bridge*? Whom was he following when, as this biographer observes, he cultivated "on principle" homosexuality and alcoholism, "cultivated them assiduously," though he did not enjoy his descent into hell and felt that he was really a martyr to it? That Crane actually "adopted" Rimbaud's "method" of living, with the same object in view, Brom Weber says, in his more recent biography of Crane,—although Rimbaud despised all the ideas that Crane was trying to realize, the Whitmanian ideas he was endeavouring to embody in *The Bridge*. Did not Rimbaud wish to "sell" democracy "if anyone would take it"? No poets were ever more antithetic in everything they had to say than Rimbaud, with his disgust for the "human pigs," for "justice, republics and peoples . . . *périssez!* . . . *passez!*" and Whitman whose whole aim was to celebrate these; and could there have been a more fatal conflict for a man who wished to sing the "Bridge,"—the "American myth,"—of which Whitman "flung the span"? Add to this that some of Crane's friends distrusted his plan for *The Bridge* partly because they themselves disliked Walt Whitman and one has what Brom Weber calls the "death wish" that was "strong within him because of his inability to defend his belief." In the face of those whom Brom Weber describes as his "intellectual and artistic mentors," who "drove" Hart Crane into a corner, he tried to "delude himself . . . with desperate hope . . . into thinking that it was he who had faith in the future." Inevitably, since faith in the future was of the essence of his theme, the poem fell apart into fragments before it was finished. How could Hart Crane have completed *The Bridge* in the spirit in which he conceived it; and how, for that matter, could he have continued to live?

Now I have only dwelt so long on the case of Rimbaud and Hart Crane because it is emblematic of many other cases in which Americans, unsure of themselves and unsure of their tradition, have literally followed strange gods to their own undoing. It is obvious that Hart Crane, in order to carry his great theme out, should have lived deeply in harmony with the whole context of his theme, should have turned a deaf ear to disbelievers in Whitman's ideas and gone his own way in defiance of the current fashion. Even following Rimbaud's wish to "invent a new poetic language" that would be "accessible to all the senses" involved him, as Philip Horton says, in a serious conflict,* and how many other American writers have been bewildered in a similar way by models who were essentially hostile to their own deepest aims. Half aware of a tradition of their own, as Hart Crane was, and prompted to write in the vein of this tradition, they were not aware of it sufficiently to withstand a fashion that opposed it in favour of totally different ideas. Too often, moreover, these ideas have had no connection with the writer's real nature or the social world

---

* "Such ambitions involved a constant pursuit of sensation, an almost exclusive cultivation of subjective states of mind, which would be scarcely compatible with the focus of attention demanded by the historical and social subject-matter of *The Bridge*."—Philip Horton, *Hart Crane: the Life of an American Poet.*

he knows and in which he has been formed. How far did Crane, for instance, understand the peculiar conditions that produced the peculiar reaction of Rimbaud's ideas?—certainly no more than Sherwood Anderson understood D. H. Lawrence's world when he lost himself, in a measure, following Lawrence. When Anderson said, "I had a world and it slipped away from me," did he know that it *might not* have slipped if he had realized the nature of his gift as a folk story-teller and rejected every influence that was incongruous with it? Was he not, in his naivety, spoiled in a way when, losing the thread of this gift, he began to see himself as the self-conscious artist, bedazzled by the circle of Gertrude Stein and what Thomas Wolfe called the "fancy" Americans, the "aesthetic Americans" who become "more 'Flauberty' than Flaubert"? How often our writers seem to suggest the theme of Henry James, the betrayal of the "innocent" American by a "corrupt" old Europe, though the Europeans would be only too happy if Americans followed their natural bent instead of tagging blindly after them.

What this means is that American writers should not only know themselves but should know the deep world of feeling that lies behind them, a world that is really different from the European world and that has shaped the images which fill their minds. They should follow every influence that fortifies these, rejecting every influence that dissipates them, as they should know the laws of the literary life and see them in the light of their own tradition. Not that they should read too much or follow American models alone,—how much Sherwood Anderson might have profited if he had studied Chekhov! And it would be impossible for teachers of literature to present too wide a range of models from the literature of the world. But is it not best, since one must have models, to have them on one's own terms, models, generally congruous with one's own conditions, who can illustrate the complex art of living as a writer and tell writers what they ought to know? These models can explain what Goethe meant when he said, "Spend not a moment's time with people to whom you do not belong and who do not belong to you," and they can show how far Virginia Woolf was right when she asked for "five hundred pounds a year and a room of one's own." They can show perhaps that the "life of pleasure" may be as "boring and painful" as it is to Aldous Huxley who has found rewarding the "narrow way of domestic duty" and "intellectual labour."

Well, then, if it has this value, is not our tradition worth exploring to find whatever models exist in the past,—that is to say, if we are able to reach the past over the war-scorched earth of the last few decades? For the world wars have disinherited innumerable sensitive American minds that have lost their sense alike of the past and the future, minds that have been conditioned, moreover, by their experience of war to a life that is not easily related to the life of our old writers. Even if there were no more wars it would take several decades for the agitated minds of the young writers of our day, accustomed to violence, excitement and perpetual movement, to see that life as anything but tedious, insipid, flat and dull. But how many good caretakers of their talents existed in that older world, in which the question of "frustration" was not omnipresent and in which there were at least a dozen writers regarding whom one could not say that they were "truncated" or "incomplete." What a wonderful example, for instance, was Hawthorne, with his four rules of life: to break off customs, to meditate on youth, to shake off spirits ill-disposed and to do nothing against one's genius. Another was Thoreau, who said that a writer should saunter to his task surrounded by a halo of ease and leisure and who showed how far a man could arrange his life to make this possible by living without impedimenta on a few cents a day. What a quarry of practical wisdom for writers lies exposed, moreover, in some of Emerson's miscellaneous papers, suggestions of every sort, tonics for the torpid mind, stimulants and purgatives for minds that are untuned or crippled. One does not recollect this to shame the present with examples of the past or to magnify the importance of these writers; but is it not worth anyone's while to examine a period in one's own past that has had such substantial consequences? Not that writers should confine their explorations to a single American region,—for one can find models now throughout the country, along with examples of the mistakes that writers fall into,—in a day when the world is all before them, where to choose, and one may find models all over the planet. The important thing is that they should transcend the juvenile roles they so often perform,—the role of the playboy, the tough guy, the groping adolescent,—in which they perpetually repeat themselves and exploit their personalities until they are as tired of themselves as we are tired of them. Only the right models, rightly chosen to fit their special aptitudes, can jog them out of these roles into which they settle, models whom they cannot "knock out of the ring" because they are a sort of superior selves, of the same nature with them but enlarged and ripened.

# CHAPTER IV

## TRANSNATIONALISM

WHY DOES ONE talk of an American tradition, dwelling upon one's country at a time when people are thinking in planetary terms, when the history of nations considered alone has come to seem parochial and only worth knowing as a chapter in the history of man? I understand the feeling that Karl Shapiro, the poet, expressed in a published letter written from an army camp, "I write about myself, my home, my street and my city, and not about 'America,' the word that is the chief enemy of modern poetry." If I were a poet I might share this feeling about a word that has been so abused, that has been spoiled perhaps for the use of a poet. There are times and seasons for everything, even times when "one's country or one's nation" seems "a brute to be kicked in the ribs," as AE put it,—that great-hearted Irishman who said, "We live by our friends, not by our country," but who had laboured for his country with devoted affection. Certainly the nationalism of which hatred and vanity are the governing traits has become in the twentieth century a planetary nuisance, and one can only hope with Renan that, after deluging the world with blood, it will vanish altogether in a few generations.

But obviously nationalism means many things to many minds,—no word has more complex implications,—and there are even communists, professing to believe in a nationless world, for whom it is not entirely obnoxious or foolish. There are times when even political nationalism seems to be a necessary step in the development of international feeling,—for instance, in the case of the colonial mind for which another nationality has an obsessive power over one's own. As a boy must react against his parents in order to become a man, so colonies must assert themselves to become nations before they can play their full part in an international order. Is this not true of all dependent states?—a fact that explains why the poet Tagore renounced his British title at the moment when the Indian people came into their own. When, only the other day, the Dutch government of Indonesia apologized for the shooting of three Indians to the government at Delhi, it was doing what it would never have done when the government at Delhi was controlled not by the Indians but by the English. Those who see as political only, and deprecate accordingly, the setting up of states like India and other new republics, fail to see what this means for the self-respect of the peoples involved as well as for their standing with other peoples. Does it not mean much for the development of literature also? It was only when Norway declared its independence of Denmark that the development of Norwegian literature began, and this led Ibsen to remark a few years later, "Culture is unthinkable apart from national life." When the sentiment of national self-respect turns into belligerent self-assertion, when pride turns into "sacred egoism," then is the time to rebuke the sentiment in question, but how right meanwhile was the old Boston essayist who based a generalization on the Greek war of independence against the Turks. No colonial or dependent people had ever possessed, he said, the requisite nobility of mind to produce great writers, and this explains why our own early writers clamoured for an American literature that was "purged of old-world influences" and all the rest. Is not Mr. Lorne Pierce similarly right in his book *A Canadian People* concerning the absence of a Canadian literature and art? He lays the blame on the intellectuals who have been the victims of an "itch for cosmopolitanism," as he puts it, suggesting that, while old and established countries can afford to cultivate this, the case is entirely different with a young small nation. "A young nation requires nothing," Mr. Pierce remarks, "so much as the simple desire to be itself." It needs to cultivate all its forces within itself. It needs for a while to cultivate a national outlook.*

* In one of the provincial capitals of Canada, I once visited the Anglican cathedral. The verger, taking me into the sacristy, showed me the relics. There were two of these, a Bible presented by King Edward VII and a fragment of the altar-cloth that was used at the coronation of King William IV. These relics of two English kings were virtually venerated as relics of saints,—or at least they filled the place of saintly relics,—and this struck me as a pathetic emblem of the colonial mind. Where such an exaggerated value attaches to another nationality, how low must be the general feeling for one's own. Never before had

There are thus evidently times and seasons when various types of nationalism have their historic use and their function to perform, and a certain kind of nationalism retains in the cultural sphere, and will always and everywhere, no doubt, retain its value. What is this nationalism, and why is even this regarded in critical circles with distrust and suspicion, so that one cannot utter a kind word for this country without being accused of waving the Stars and Stripes? I suggest that, on a larger scale, it is identical with the regionalism that William Faulkner champions in *Intruder in the Dust,* wishing to defend his little nation against what he calls "the North," which consists for him merely of "rootless ephemeral cities." He says that in the South alone one finds the homogeneity from which anything of durable value comes for a people; and if the "outland," the rest of America, were truly what he feels it is, one would also be obliged, like Faulkner, to "defy" it. But, while it is far from possessing the homogeneity a country should have, can it really be described in such terms as ephemeral and rootless? If, as Faulkner says, literature, art and science are the durable fruits of homogeneity, the nation is more than the sum of its mushroom cities,— it must be homogeneous too, in some essential way, and proportionally in a fuller sense than any of its parts. That it possesses some homogeneity virtually every American feels in the fact that, for him, his country is the focus of emotions that homelands are

I so clearly understood what the Revolution had done for the American mind.

for people everywhere, the centre of the circle that Rebecca West described, in *The Meaning of Treason,* from which "we have forgotten that we live outward. . . . What is nearest to the centre," she adds, "is most real to us."

Many have forgotten this because people are so largely urbanized now, because of the multiplicity of their social contacts, because they are surrounded in towns by others whose circumstances they do not know, with whom they possess few memories and associations in common. They are like Willa Cather's Linstrom,* lost fragments of humanity, rolling stones, who have no ties, no local habitations, who have lost the feeling for the nation and the race that village folk retain in their long common experience and recollection. In losing this they have lost their feeling for certain basic vital truths that deepen the personality, as Lewis Mumford puts it, for certain energies, certain vitalities that underlie the conscious life and connect the individual with the life of nature. Has not this been especially true of the intellectuals who are so

---

* "Here you are an individual, you have a background of your own, you would be missed. But off there in the cities there are thousands of rolling stones like me. We are all alike,—we have no ties, we know nobody, we own nothing. When one of us dies, they scarcely know where to bury him. Our landlady and the delicatessen man are our mourners, and we leave nothing behind us but a frock-coat and a fiddle, or an easel or a typewriter, or whatever tool we get our living by. We live in the streets, in the parks, in the theatre. We sit in restaurants and concert halls and look about at the hundreds of our own kind and shudder."—Carl Linstrom to Alexandra, in Willa Cather's *O Pioneers!*

largely drawn from urban populations and who carry on, to their great disadvantage,—to the great disadvantage of others too,—a life that is wholly unrelated to the life of the people? Inevitably, therefore, the intellectuals discredit nationalism in every form, supposing that nationalism and imperialism are interchangeable notions, and regarding it as a mere superstition that one should be expected to care more for one's own country than for any other. And yet, while their country leaves them cold, how many of these intellectuals have been filled with patriotic fervour in connection with France, the traditional homeland of artists which stirs in them a feeling like the feeling that Russia excites in the Stalinite breast. What a cry went up in June, 1942, when one first heard of the French collaborationist artists. It was reported that Derain, Vlaminck, Despiau and others were travelling and lecturing in Germany as guests of Hitler (for when artists are "above" politics they are apt to lend themselves to politics that first destroy their country and presently themselves). Then one heard intellectuals saying, No, this could not be true! It could not be true of this one or of that one,—how could Derain betray France?—for France to these intellectuals possessed the mystical value that America lacked. They were as conventionally patriotic as any villager could be, once their group-feeling for a nation was fully aroused.

But there are numbers of reasons why the intellectuals have only negative feelings about nationalism, any kind, even the valuable kind that is concerned with culture alone and has little to do with politics or nothing whatever. One is the communist-mindedness that was so prevalent in the past and that sees in any defence of a nation an attempt to set up again an obsolete tribal pattern of outmoded feeling. Another is the general negativism that is so common in our day and sees only propaganda in any cause, in any positive statement of any group-feeling, while there is a special negativism, with a long history for writers, that considers any feeling for America as somehow tainted. This is the "exile's" point of view, established among the Expatriates by the influences that played over their minds in the nineteen-twenties, first by the critics of that time who largely repudiated American life and secondly by the writers who surrounded them in Europe. The exiles one and all rebelled against the banalities of the United States, as Mencken and Sinclair Lewis, among others, revealed them, establishing in their minds the feeling that life in their own country, for the writer and artist at least, was not worth living. Ezra Pound, Eliot and Gertrude Stein implied this also by living abroad, while Joyce, D. H. Lawrence and many another renounced in the same way their native lands. What followed was the negativism, in virtually all that concerned America, of the most influential group of American writers, among them Hemingway, who could see "nobility and dignity" in the Spanish people but seldom seemed to see it in his own. Only unfashionable writers like Sandburg could see nobility and dignity at home, as most of the writers had seen it a century before, well knowing that human beings are much the same in every country but having an affection for their own. So it was natural that a whole generation of writers should have grown up for whom any feeling for America was chauvinistic and who were confirmed in their negativism by the sense of living in a meaningless world that was induced by a chronic state of war. They inherited disinheritance, as one might put it.

What then am I defending when I seem to speak kindly of nationalism, which in most of the usual senses cannot be defended, in our planetary twentieth-century world when all the great spirits of the time are in favour of lowering the barriers between the nations? How can one speak for parochial ideas when, reading a book about Bali, one uses as a bookmark a postcard from a friend in New Zealand and when the book in question was written in four countries, Norway, Sweden, Italy and England? How can anyone speak parochially in a world of soldiers who have seen service in France, in the South Pacific, in the Hebrides, Africa, Sicily, Guadalcanal, in a world, moreover, of displaced persons like the intellectuals whom we know, from every country, who are living a nomad's life? One and all have learned to say, "My country is the world," with Thomas Paine and Dante long before him, and in fact we are all obliged to speak for the universal, the planetary man, feeling that more restricted categories are out of the question. We agree with Burckhardt that "historical judgment" should be "of such a nature that all nations, if not all parties, could subscribe to it," that the world is a whole and that we are of this whole, though this whole does not necessarily efface the part. For is one necessarily less pan-human because one happens to be something particular as well? Indeed, the word international implies the preservation of nationalities that have learned how to exist side by side. Because we are of the planet, can we not also be not only of the country but of the village, living from within outward in concentric circles,—cherishing Kipling's "one spot . . . beloved above all," although "God gave all men all earth to love"? Did not Dante, while saying "My country is the world," find a new home as it were in the language of Italy that in a sense he created,—quoting the phrase of Cicero, "nearness begets friendship," which is all one needs to say for nationalism? And what is lost and how much is gained in the fact that in Alan Paton's novel Africa appears as the "beloved country"? Does the cry "God save Africa" exclude the planet in focussing a particular feeling on one salvable part? This is indeed the common cry among the ripe-hearted in every country for whom their own people are emblems of the rest of mankind, for whom charity begins at home,—and, if it does not begin at home, it will almost certainly never begin at all. Who can object to an English novel in which one character says to another, "This is a beautiful country, is it not?"— a feeling from which countless English writers have gained a warmth and depth which all the intelligence in the world cannot impart. Then why should this feeling with us be regarded with suspicion?

Not that our drastic critical movement of thirty years

ago was not both warranted and salutary,—it surely was so; and the reason it aroused so many writers was that so much warmth and faith lay, perhaps invisibly, behind it. It was only the first world war that carried this movement to the negative degree of nihilism; and in any case this tide has long since turned. It turned, at least in certain minds, with what has been called the failure of Europe, which made many writers think better of this country; and Sandburg's great life of Lincoln was only one of a multitude of books that expressed a new sense of "the ground we stand on." This tendency made Henry Miller's *Air-Conditioned Nightmare* seem curiously anachronistic when it finally appeared, when, brought home "like a runaway slave," Miller set out on his nightmarish tour through the "damned hole" of the Holland Tunnel. Since tunnels are necessarily "holes" and, of all possible tunnels, the Holland Tunnel is surely the least "damned," one saw how the cards were stacked for Miller,—and how he was predisposed to see "all the streets of America combined" as "forming a huge cesspool of the spirit." One could only say further about this book that his feeling left no scope for a talent that had found in Greece a congenial theme, though this talent revealed itself in one fine chapter about a plantation-house in Louisiana. Others found it natural to follow the prescription of William James on returning to America from Europe, to "pitch one's whole sensibility first in a different key," though the moment of change might be "lonesome." Then "gradually," as James said, "the quantum of personal happiness of which one is susceptible fills the cup," and certainly for many writers this quantum of personal happiness was more and more identified with affection for the country. Which of them did not, and does not, feel at least a touch of personal pride in the fact that Thoreau influenced Gandhi, or in the fact that writers as different as Tolstoy, Yeats and Proust were in one way or another moved by *Walden?* Who does not find pleasure in the feeling that Shaw was right when he said, "America is at last producing an art of its own instead of merely boring Europe by returning its exports with all their charm rubbed off"? But have not Europeans always wished Americans to do this? What was the word among English critics more than a hundred years ago when the "father of American poetry" appeared in England?—that he was not "sufficiently American" to suit them; and this was what Goethe meant when he regretted that Washington Irving abandoned American for European themes. He liked Cooper better for writing American romances. Did not Emerson observe that "genuine growths" like the journals of Western pioneers were "sought with avidity in Europe, where our European-like books are of no value"?—and may one not say that in general the writers of every country who most interest others are those in whom one most feels the uniqueness of their country? Does not the whole world delight in the Spanishness of *Don Quixote,* the Englishness of *As You Like It* and the Germanness of *Faust?* Granting the important qualification that other things are equal, is this not what foreigners seek most in us, and quite as truly in the days of Hem-

ingway and Faulkner as they sought it in the days of
Cooper, Thoreau and Hawthorne?

But few will question the actuality or the value of
this nationalism so long as one speaks of the "golden
world" of letters, the phrase in which Sir Philip Sidney
differentiated the poets' world from the "brazen
world" of nature and every day. Few will dispute what
Poe called *"that* nationality which defends our own
literature, sustains our own men of letters, upholds
our own dignity and depends upon our own resources." We have always had to affirm this, though
surely not so much today as in the days when Americans only saw this country when they could see it as
European,* and, like the English of Shakespeare's
time, in the words of Thomas Morley, could esteem
only what came "from beyond the seas." † This kind
of nationalism a critic is bound to affirm, the nationalism of the poets, novelists and thinkers, a golden world
in which one finds neither Roman, Jew, Barbarian

* How characteristic of American feeling as late as 1880 was
the note struck in the lines that follow, taken from an old paper
on the artists of East Hampton, Long Island: "To Abbey, the
gardens, the lawns, the shrubbery were pure English. The mead-
ows, the salt marshes, the dunes and windmills brought Holland to Frost. Bolton Jones found Brittany here, and Bruce
Crane was carried straight to Pont-Aven by the hayricks, the
poultry yards, the winding sheep, the returning herds lost in a
haze of soft grey atmosphere so like their beloved Barbizon."

† ". . . The incurable bias of our cultured and leisured classes
who, as Thomas Morley observed at the close of the sixteenth
century, 'highly esteem whatever cometh from beyond the seas,
and especially from Italy, be it never so simple, condemning that
which is done at home, though it be never so excellent'."—A. K.
Holland, *Henry Purcell.*

nor Greek, for the prejudices of the brazen world are left behind there. There whatever can be called human is judged on its merits alone because it is judged in the light of the imagination,—one has to apologize there for subhuman opinions; and this little republic that mirrors in its way the great republic of unimaginative minds always relates *what is* to *what ought to be*. To this world one can give one's full allegiance assured that by so doing one cannot betray anything that is good or worthy, for it is an over-world that parallels the over-world of the Christian faith in which there is nothing common or unclean.

To affirm this is not to defend the sadly different brazen world in which we spend most of our days, a world to which, in large part, a critic must be hostile if he is to play his role in the golden world. One does not have to call America, with Henry Miller, "this null-and-void . . . producing the greatest misery of the greatest number," to be aware of its moral drop in the eyes of other peoples who spoke of it once as "the lodge of humanity in the West." For anyone to whom it appears that this country stands chiefly for the power of money, what irony it is to think of the divines of old who prayed that their descendants might never be rich, or even of the day when, without a blush, George Ticknor could say to a Grand Duke of Tuscany that America was "more elevating than other countries." Who can be happy that, in France, America is the country of Richard Wright's *Native Son* and *Black Boy,* in which Negroes are shot like blackbirds in trees or given knives, to fight one another, like gamecocks, for the amusement of Tennessee whites? Or the country of Erskine Caldwell's stories in which sheriffs go fishing when lynchings occur and "nigger hunting" and "possum hunting" are on the same level? Then was it not an American whom André Gide refused to meet because he boasted of eating human flesh in the days when his once puritanical countrymen offended the simple Majorcans with their ostentatious nakedness and tasteless pleasures? How childish Americans are, moreover, erecting a statue to Popeye, or permitting the spinach-raisers to erect one in Texas, because this tough-guy sailor advertised spinach, or allowing themselves to be carried away so far by competitive sport that the West Point military academy was demoralized by it. H. G. Wells's phrase for America, "The great problem child of humanity," was plausibly matched by his remark that the spirit of the country was as unstable as a monkey's,—as inquisitive and lively,—because Americans never read books and only read headlines in newspapers, a statement that could not have been made a hundred years ago. For how marked has been the deterioration of culture in a country in which hundreds of thousands now pass each year through college. An English librarians' committee recently reported the remark of an American who visited England in 1849: "Nothing strikes an American more forcibly than to see how little reading there is in England." A century later, as everyone knows, it is four to one the other way. Four books are published in England to every one in the United States,—that is to say, in proportion to the population,

—while America is known the world over mainly for what, if not its cheap comic books and commercialized movies?

Is there anything, in fact, in our brazen world that a serious writer can defend unless he regards the idea that lies behind it, an idea that has lain behind the country consistently for so long a time that one can virtually identify the idea with the country? One may take as a symbol of this the fact that, in 1915, dreaming of a "colony of escape from ruined Europe," and hoping to plant the seed of a more creditable world, D. H. Lawrence proposed to settle in Florida to do it. He urged Katherine Mansfield and Middleton Murry to foster with him there the "germ of a new era," as he called it,—the "uncreated future, the unborn, the unconceived,"—because there was a "living sky" above America and all there was not "destruction and dying and corruption." Was this not precisely the idea of Coleridge and Southey a century before when they planned their Pantisocracy on the Susquehanna, as of Bishop Berkeley a century earlier still when he looked for his golden age also in the west? And of William Penn fifty years earlier than Berkeley? One and all were illustrating the old American messianic belief that this country was divinely appointed to deliver the world from European inequality, intolerance and corruption, as well as from the squalor and darkness of Africa and Asia, the theme of so many orations and sermons a hundred years ago that was also the theme of Hart Crane's unachieved epic. It was in the spirit of this belief that the immigrants came for so many generations to escape from the inequalities, intolerances and corruptions of Europe, so many kinds of immigrants that the country became in time "the place where a Cosmopolis is being tried out." Wyndham Lewis, saying this, amplifies the phrase by adding that America is "the ante-chamber of a world-state." He might have added furthermore that it appears to be the place where the planetary mind is at last emerging.

It would be very surprising if, in advance of other folk, Americans did not develop the planetary mind, for as many races have been dissolved in the American population as there were in the crew of the "Pequod" in *Moby-Dick*. How symbolic of the coming America the "Pequod" was, in point of fact, with its company of English, Dutch, Irish and Portuguese sailors, and sailors from Sicily, Iceland, Denmark and Spain, as numerous and varied as the racial types that appeared in *Leaves of Grass*, which was also, a century ago, prophetic of the present. Whitman had seen many of these types in America, and he felt about all the peoples of "the great round wonder rolling through space" as no poet had ever felt before him. For, even disregarding the local implication, what poet in the older countries *could* have exclaimed, "Health to you! Good will to you all, from me and America sent!"

The Irish writer AE, whom I have quoted so often and who had the intuitive faculty that is called prophetic, observed more than once that Americans were the first people to adopt a planetary point of view or frame of mind. "You have a vision about this planet that no other nation has ever had," he said to an

American ambassador a few years ago, indicating what this implied, that the Americans were getting ready to assume responsibilities involving all mankind. But long before this he had written that in Whitman, Emerson and Thoreau, more than in any European writers of their time, one found "the dawning of something which might be spoken of as cosmic or planetary consciousness." These were the writers who formed, as he put it, the "germ-cell of American culture," and they were the writers in whom he seemed to see the starting-point of the world-culture of the future, while, as for Emerson, we know that he developed the planetary mind in part to escape from a colonial relationship to England. No one could have been more aware of what he called the "tyranny of the British element" in American culture, to "resist" which, he said in *English Traits,* "a serious man must aid himself" by comparing the remotest civilizations with it. It was one of his obvious motives in studying the poetry of Arabia and Persia to escape from the sway of the whole European tradition, from the literatures of Europe that seemed "partial and clannish" to Thoreau as well when he had steeped himself in the sacred books of Asia. Beside these the European writers, to Thoreau, seemed provincial, and he rebuked them for their presumption in speaking for the world when really they spoke for only a small corner of it. If the planetary mind is developing here, these older writers might be said to have formed its "germ-cell" on the literary level; and Ezra Pound was their successor when he refused to recognize what he called "parochial borders to the artistic tradition."

It would certainly not be true to say that, generally speaking, world-culture has ever been assimilated here as deeply as in Europe, but Americans, always so relatively weak in their time-sense, or sense of the past, have recently gained the space-sense to an immeasurable degree. I mean that sense of the planet as a whole, a certain all-world-mindedness beside which many Europeans seem provincially complacent, assuming that world-civilization is European or nothing, or nothing if it is not German or English or French. Whatever can be said of American complacency—and how much must be said!—there is much to be said of American humility also, not the "difficult" virtue that Eliot talks of but the quality of eager simple folk who have gone to school to Europe for three hundred years. What they have learned by, that they have grown by, as the Egyptologist Breasted learned and grew, the prairie boy, the druggist's apprentice who had to expose in the end what he called "the fallibility of old-world scholarship" in Maspero and Petrie. If Americans have risen in the scholarly world it is because they were humble so long, aware that they were provincials who must learn at the centre, just as their multiracial state compelled them to trace out the principles by which peoples can get along together. It is no accident that all the sciences which are devoted to discovering these,—anthropology, sociology, psychology, semantics,—should have become American studies,

or largely so, of late, as Stuart Chase points out in
*The Proper Study of Mankind.*

For how could American society function at all if
it had not developed the interracial mind?—the cause
or the effect, and possibly both, of what Wyndham
Lewis calls the American "impulse to befriend . . .
to treat all men as brothers"? One sees in the novels
of the second world war how readily the American
soldier finds buddies in men of all races under the
sun; and has not the American reportage of the world
war epoch revealed a similar aptitude in journalism
also? When one thinks of the pre-world-war corre-
spondents who were so generally of the type of the socially irresponsible romantic soldier of fortune, how
can one sufficiently mark the difference in men like
John Gunther or Shirer or Swing, Louis Fischer, Vin-
cent Sheean or Louis Adamic? Sometimes on the level
of literature proper, as John Reed may be said to
have been in *Ten Days That Shook the World* and,
far more so, John Hersey in *The Wall* and *Hiroshima,*
they have had in common a profound concern for the
well-being of alien races, with a deep intuitive understanding of them. Waldo Frank in *America Hispaña*
and *South American Journey* is a marked case in
point; and these writers have judged their alien peoples not in a locally American way but rather with a
distinct all-human feeling. Does this not suggest the
identification of the speaker with the spoken of that
Dostoievsky claimed as a trait of the Russians? De-
scribing, in his speech on Pushkin, what he called
the Russian soul as omni-human and all-uniting,

dwelling on its tendency to universal sympathy, he said that to be a true Russian meant to "aspire to reconcile the contradictions of Europe." But perhaps "to pronounce the final word of the great general harmony," not of Europe only but of the world, may be the role of the nation that is made up of so many nations and is really already an emblem of the world-state to come.

One might mention other reasons for the growth in the United States of the sort of planetary-mindedness that is requisite for this, the multitudinous flight, for one, of the bright minds of the old world who have settled in the most unlikely corners of the country. Have we not seen whole faculties of Central European universities transported bodily and reëstablished here, along with philosophers, novelists, musicians, architects, chemists, psychologists, painters who have widened on every hand the local horizon? * They have found themselves in a world that is too fluid for European categories, which have lost all sharpness of outline in the American air, so that phrases like "middle class," "bourgeois," "proletariat" no longer correspond with the kind of substantial realities they have

* Cf. Paul Valéry (*Reflections on the World Today*): "Whenever my thoughts become too gloomy and whenever I despair of Europe, I can restore some degree of hope only by thinking of the New World . . . Europe has sent there the communicable creations of its mind, all the most positive things it has discovered . . . It was truly a form of 'natural selection' that took place and which extracted from the European mind its products of universal value, while all its more conventional and too historical elements remained in the Old World."

known in Europe. What they find here, in fact, is not so much a nation, in the old European sense, as a state of mind, or, to quote Wyndham Lewis again, a "human laboratory" precisely "for the manufacture of cosmic man." They find an "eclectic, non-national, internationally-minded creature, whose blood is drawn—more or less—from all the corners of the earth," together with "the great promiscuous grave into which tumble and there disintegrate all that was race, class or nationhood." It seems to me that Wyndham Lewis expresses in these images, if not the reality of America, a tendency in it that constantly approaches reality, day by day, a tendency of which Frank Lloyd Wright's "open plan" in architecture might in a fashion serve as a visible symbol. For this abolishes all the partitions that have divided room from room, the privities along with the distinctions of the functions of the household, as the other abolishes the barriers between man and man in the interest of a wide sociality and all-human freedom. Wright has translated Walt Whitman into architecture.

Now just as the lover of privacy, or the introvert, as one might say, feels that all he values would be lost if he had to adjust himself to this "open" setting, so the lover of the old racial state shudders at the prospect of an "open" world in which race, class and nationhood have so largely vanished. There is something in every man that longs for the *piccolo mondo antico,* the little old group-culture, cosily warm, to which every generation looks back as a paradise lost, the accustomed cells from which humanity is always being drawn away by the forces of a larger, barer and more general existence. Much is always lost as one phase of history moves into another, as Europe lost much in emerging from the Middle Ages, the spirituality, for one example, of the fourteenth-century Madonna of art when she developed into the earthy human mother. But, whatever losses the process involves,—and these will never prove to be as catastrophic as many anticipate at present, inasmuch as men themselves will not cease to be human,—must we not, at any cost, realize the "one world" that we now possess the means to bring about? Have we any choice if the alternative is world destruction? And what has made possible this realization if not the "open society" that has produced in America the planetary mind, the kind of society, safe for differences, promoting, not unity, based on repression, but the highest degree of diversity, the result of freedom? As for this open society itself, it could only have come about through the liberal-democratic ideas of the age of revolutions, the ideas of the Enlightenment, based on a belief in men, that many describe as "illusions" in our generation. These are the ideas that animated Jefferson, Emerson, Lincoln, Melville and Whitman, the minds that have peculiarly expressed the uniqueness of this country; and can they truly be called illusions if the future of the world *depends upon their proving to be real?* How, moreover, can they be "refuted," as people say they have been today, if they stand for the values that humanity *wishes to retain,* true as it is that the nature of man is more complex than many supposed in the age of faith that was also the age of revolutions?

So the defence of nationalism turns out to be, in American terms, really a defence of Whitman's "orbic" mind, with a defence of the Revolution that stood for the emergence of a "new man" out of the old shell of the parochial sectarian European. But in presupposing the abolition of political sovereignties, more and more, it also presupposes the maintaining of the cultures of the world, of every positive cultural trait that serves to enrich the general life, beginning, in each people, with its own.

# CHAPTER V

## THE SILENT GENERATION

So MUCH FOR the ideas that have made an "open society" possible,—and where does one hear a good word for them today? Who speaks of the humanitarian, the liberal, the progressive, *without* which we could never have attained the planetary mind? Have they not become, universally, bywords, symbols of all that is beneath contempt in respectable critical circles both in America and England, as if there were some positive virtue in moving backward like the crab and averting one's eyes from the hopes and the miseries of the world? Among those who speak our tongue today one finds few critics of any weight for whom these once-poignant words deserve respect or who do not unite in the general praise of reaction, authority, hierarchy, order, as if "closed" societies were preferable to those that are "open." Who finds anyone to agree with the novelist James A. Michener that "we must announce our loyalty . . . now more than ever . . . to those religious, political and humanitarian principles which seem best calculated to see a man or a nation through a period of darkness"? For what is the task of a novelist at such a moment in history?—Mr. Michener enquires in *The Arts in Renewal;* and he says it is "to remind all men of those well-springs of humanism that have nourished our society in the past." He continues: "The tragedy is that now, when the liberal tradition should be supporting these aspirants, it is everywhere in cowardly retreat." In fact, "we are witnessing," he adds, "a concerted attempt to drive America from the open highway of liberalism and into a retreat toward the caves of an all-powerful reaction."

Can this be disputed by anyone who has followed the trend of the most powerful school of contemporary critics, for whom, as Mr. Ransom says, "the word for our generation is 'formal'" and might be further qualified as "reactionary"? For these critics, Mr. Ransom observes, the "gospel of progress" is a "curious development" and one to be extinguished as soon as may be,—that "easy optimistic gospel of roaring irresistible movement to Utopia" to which another critic of our day refers. One remembers little that was "irresistible," little that was "easy" and nothing that "roared" in Professor J. B. Bury's "Idea of Progress,"—which remained an affirmative conception, none the less,—but let that pass while one returns to other contemporary critical minds who agree with Mr. Ransom in this region of ideas. Everyone knows Mr. Eliot's views on "programmes, platforms, scientific progress, humanitarianism and revolutions which improved nothing,"—conceptions that make "damnation" seem sweet to him,—and liberalism is "desperately weak" for Lionel Trilling because it cannot face the wickedness of man. For the same reason Reinhold Niebuhr believes that our liberal culture is too superficial and blind to direct an age that must build a new system on the ruins of an old one, although, "right wing" in his religion, he is "left wing" in politics and opposed to the "closed society" that so many desire. For, according to Auden, an "increasing number of people" are coming to believe that an "open society" is impossible because men are so wicked; and, for them, the only escape from disaster is to return, as Auden says, to a closed type of society with all possible speed.* While Auden, like Niebuhr, dissociates himself from this widespread movement of our time, he denies in his philosophy the faith in the capacities of men without which no open society could ever have arisen, reviving, with Niebuhr and Eliot and Ransom, the idea of "original sin" and the "natural bias" of all men "to do evil." Is it not what might be called this newly changed notion of human nature, or, rather, this recent return to the mediæval notion,—that men are more radically evil than potentially good,—is it not this notion which has spread through the world in the last three decades that has caused the movement of reaction? And perhaps this is natural at a time when the Yahoo element in men has been more vociferous and active than for many generations.

---

* "The failure of the human race to acquire the habits that an open society demands if it is to function properly, is leading an increasing number of people to the conclusion that an open society is impossible, and that, therefore, the only escape from economic and spiritual disaster is to return as quickly as possible to a closed type of society."—W. H. Auden, *Criticism in a Mass Society*, in *The Intent of the Critic*, edited by Donald A. Stauffer.

But when one considers that the liberal experiment is scarcely two hundred years old and has only been tried in a small minority of nations, one might think it premature to give this up so suddenly because the *bête humaine* has come to the front. It seems still more premature considering what closed societies are, as we have seen them at work in our own time, the closed societies of Hitler and Stalin, not to mention Franco Spain, where no one knows the writers because they cannot be published. In Spain, Protestant churches are burned with impunity, but, holding the ideas they do, how can our reactionary critics object to this, any more than the reigning European writers of the last few decades could have objected to it either? For whatever one thinks of their ideas, who questions the supremacy in talent of Proust, Joyce, D. H. Lawrence, Eliot and Yeats, the rulers of the literary mind of the last generation?—and all of them despised the humanitarian liberalism that alone has kept our society hitherto open. Since they despised its aspirations *with* its actualities, they raise the question whether we must choose between our beliefs and a measure of sympathy with *them,* for obviously we must decide which tendency we are to follow, the ideas of these writers or the liberalism they reject and oppose. This, for the moment, is beside the question. It is beside the question that these writers have repudiated liberalism root and branch, wishing to see it abolished altogether. What is to the point is that they have sanctioned and partly created the "reactionary programmes" that our colleges today are "fabricating." I quote these phrases from Harry Levin, who says that, "abhorring thought-control," we are nevertheless "hankering after conformity today . . . Traditionally . . . we find ourselves committed to experiment, exploration, examination, progression, and from time to time subversion," while "our younger voices, which ought in the course of nature to be radical," seem generally to have turned the other way. They "exhort us to revisit conservatism, to vitalize the centre, to do penance for the sins of the liberal imagination." *

No doubt this academic tendency is due, in part at least, to a fear of communism that breeds the conservative mind, as the reactionary tendency of the European writers is deeply connected with the exhaustion, the diminution of Europe. But the question is why the ideas of these writers have acquired such an influence in a world that is deeply committed not to hold them, the liberal-democratic American world in which the critics more and more find themselves in harmony with these ideas. Is the fear of communism wholly or mainly the cause of this? Or is it mainly perhaps the fear of

* Harry Levin, *The Tradition of Tradition*, in *The Hopkins Review*, Spring, 1951.
Cf. R. H. Robbins (*The T. S. Eliot Myth*): "In the West,"—the Western world,—"particularly in America, control of the press, the chairs at the universities, the memberships on prize committees, etc., of all that determines the shaping of opinion and the making of reputations, has come into the hands of conservatives."

As Auden says in *The Age of Anxiety*:

> The decent advice
> of the liberal weeklies [is] as lost an art
> as peasant pottery.

freedom of which we have also heard so much, the half-conscious flight from the heavy burden of individual choice that a free society places on its members? Are men weary of their inability to solve their own problems? Are they tired of being themselves or of going forward, so that they are eager for passivity and relish defeat, embracing the "apathy, uninventiveness and inertia" through which, for E. M. Forster, "the best chance for future society lies"? Any of these motives might account for what Harry Levin calls "our heresy-hunting critical tradition-mongers"; for one and all are elements of what used to be called the spirit of the age, or what might be called at present its want of spirit.

One's own time is always the obscurest epoch. As Logan Pearsall Smith observed, "We are the children of our age but children who can never know their mother." Who, moreover, can be said to represent an age? Not the grandfathers or the children but the middle generation. It is understood in the literary world that every writer has his day and stands as it were on sufferance when he enters another, when he attempts to speak for, or even speak of, a later day in which a younger generation rules. Writers who grew up in the pre-war time must realize that, entering the post-war time, they enter it as visiting foreigners who are intelligent, perhaps, but by no means the natives who are qualified to express it directly; and yet, still living in this post-war time, they can still claim to be of it and are bound to unriddle it also as well as they can. For must we not all, for our own satisfaction, elicit some pattern from our world, although this may well be a false simplification, attempting to see in it what will be seen a generation hence by other intelligent foreigners looking backward? And how can we characterize this age of earthquake weather, the "age of anxiety," as it is often called,* in which William Faulkner says, quite simply, "There is only one question, When will I be blown up"? Faulkner continues, "Our tragedy today is a general and universal physical fear so long sustained by now that we can bear it." And is this not a perceptive diagnosis? But that people can bear this fear does not change the fact that it plays havoc with their minds, their nerves, their hearts.

Is this not one obvious explanation of many of the elements of our age, the notes that especially mark the literary mind and what H. G. Wells called the "frightful queerness" that has come into modern life, in which people once more openly speak of the Devil? The highly intuitive Gertrude Stein also said that life today had ceased to be "real" and become "strange,"—so what was the use any longer of being "realistic"?—and does not this strangeness or queerness, whatever its cause, define the dominant interests and tastes of the day? Does not something in it explain the vogue of the authors who have moulded or expressed its mind, from Joyce, Rilke, Kafka or Eliot to Hemingway and Faulkner,—as well as the choice of the present in reviving from the past the writers who are somehow

* "The natural role of the twentieth-century man is anxiety," says the General in Norman Mailer's *The Naked and the Dead;* and how often one finds this repeated in contemporary writing.

harmonious with them? For is it not true that we can describe every age in terms of the new writers it produces and the old writers it revives, who are never quite the same as the writers who were cherished in the previous age, any more than the new writers who expressed it? Why should John Donne, Flaubert, Dostoievsky, Baudelaire and Rimbaud have taken the places that were occupied fifty years ago by Balzac, Victor Hugo and Tolstoy, for example, as Melville supplanted Whitman as a focus of interest and as Henry Adams supplanted William James? To ask this question is to characterize the pre-war generation in contrast to the post-war world in which we live and which seems almost to have made its own, along with surrealism and abstract art, the monstrous visions of "Hell" Breughel and Hieronymus Bosch. Why are the bewilderment, the frustration, the tension that accompany the feeling of queerness and strangeness, and that are generally recognized as notes of the day, accompanied as well by a widespread tendency to retrospection in every form, the "remembrance of things past" in one's childhood or the Middle Ages? Much of this surely expresses the feeling that the present is intolerable, too painful to be endured or at least to be thought of; and does not the hero of Dos Passos's *Chosen Country* explain this in much the same way as Faulkner? Jay Pignatelli is planning to write a book "On the Influence of War in Twentieth-Century Civilization." And indeed what an unheard of thing is a thirty-year world-war-mindedness in which virtually every young man on the planet is involved, accompanied by the atom-bomb that has made, in the twentieth century, the end of the world seem as imminent as it seemed in the tenth.

It is true that one has to ask the question whether this post-war frame of mind is not rather the effect of a pre-war sickness, the "sickness of being man" that one young poet speaks of and that was felt already in the pre-war epoch. Many writers in 1910 were saying "The human race sinks towards oblivion," a phrase of Kenneth Rexroth forty years later, and Robinson Jeffers was ready to suggest giving one's heart to the hawks, for "humanity" was "the mould to break away from." Did not *The Waste Land,* Proust's great novel, Joyce's *Ulysses* and *The Decline of the West* express the mood of world-disintegration, along with Picasso's pictures, of the pre-war time, when Thomas Mann was at work on *The Magic Mountain,* in which a sanitarium stood for the world? Which character in this was not a type of what has so often been called the sick paranoiac century we have all come to know, in which Albert Ryder's lonely boats at night on an empty stormy sea, under black flying clouds, have been a powerful symbol? In that pre-war time there were many who could say, with Alfred Hayes in his *Welcome to the Castle,* "Do not ask me what my generation can have faith in or hope for." But at least in their vision of the world the beloved was not "tumbril bait," as the young girl seemed to the old colonel in Hemingway's novel. Nor did young men typically feel as so many feel in our world-war time what the soldier Wilson says in *The Naked and the Dead,* "Goddam

carrion, that's all we are, men, goddam carrion,"—
which might almost be called a normal feeling at a
time whose recurrent refrain is Auden's "Many have
perished; more will." How naturally, moreover, the
magnetic setting of Auden's *The Age of Anxiety*,—as
of so many modern plays and stories,—is the saloon
where business looks up for the barman "when necessity is associated with horror and freedom with bore-
dom." There are always "enough lonelies" then who
need what the barman has to give,—the "sad haunters
of Perhaps" who, "estranged" and "aloof . . . brood
over being till the bar closes."

Why should one look further to account for the failure of nerve that has often been attributed to this
generation, in which Faulkner somewhere identifies
"being alive" with "an agony of naked inanaesthetiz-
able nerve-ends"? In a virtually chronic state of war,
regarding which millions have lost any clear conception of the whys and wherefores but which keeps them
nevertheless in a chronic state of tension, how can they
look forward with assurance or about them either?
The world for them is a Faulknerian world of violence
and terror, like the flood on the Mississippi in *The
Old Man,* invisible in the dark night, in the seething
gut between dizzy banks, and filled with a debris of
destruction. Objects nameless and enormous strike at
the skiff, while water-snakes out of the foam slither
over the gunwales, and how many others feel like the
anonymous Negro,—"Cast upon a medium I was born
to fear, to fetch up at last in a place I never saw before
and where I do not even know where I am." Are they

not even inclined to feel like this convict who has escaped and whose only wish, after heroically delivering his charge, is to escape back to prison? For prison is the one security that he has ever known. He refuses every chance to get away; for, rather than face freedom in the world that he has known, he prefers the "monastic existence of shotguns and shackles."

In the so-called "silent generation" that has followed the "lost generation" and that sometimes appears to be immobilized, so negative it is,—or strikes so many witnesses, at least, as being,—this might well pass for a symbol of the need for security at any price, a need that marks our time of suspended animation. The time seems too much for the individual, who has perhaps been conditioned by war to regard his own difference from others as a handicap and hindrance and who has adapted himself fatalistically to the "common denominator techniques" that suppress all originality in the army.* That individuality is benumbed or dead in countless numbers of the silent generation, who have no personal ambition or desire for adventure or any wish to speak out for anything,—for they have no militant beliefs,—competent observers have reported. Why go in for social agitation when slums are on the way out and rising wages are abolishing the old exploited classes?—while the fear of being "subversive"

* "In the army the idea of individual personality is just a hindrance. Sure, there are differences among men in any particular army, but they invariably cancel each other out, and what you're left with is a value rating . . . I work with grosser techniques, common denominator techniques."—The General in Norman Mailer's *The Naked and the Dead*.

is only equalled by an all but universal desire to "conform." That war is by no means the only cause of this passive point of view, that it merely confirms the results of other causes, might be the conclusion of any reader of Erich Fromm and his disquieting book *Escape from Freedom*. How convincingly Fromm explains the feelings of insecurity, powerlessness, fear and personal insignificance that modern life breeds, together with the modern industrial system that engenders internal compulsions and restraints which prevent the individual from using his freedom. Democracy frees him from external restraints, but what value has this freedom if he cannot establish his own individual existence?—and gigantic forces in the outer world play upon him constantly and destroy his personal judgment and his personal feeling. The vastness of modern cities, the mountainlike buildings, the radio, the newspaper headlines perpetually changing create a mass-mindedness in him that reduces to nothing his sense of himself in a world to which he might otherwise have felt he belonged. His freedom then tends to become an intolerable burden, and, as eager to escape from it as his fathers had been to fight for it, he finds a new security in one of two fashions. Uniting with others who feel equally powerless and alone, he seeks for a leader who will give him the word of command, or he conforms with any process in which he can lose himself,—and, if he becomes an automaton, so much the better.

Does this not explain some of the symptoms of the "silent generation," those who are said to be only happy when they are members of a "group," since they have no wish to act or think alone? And how much more natural this is when so many feel they are fated to die in a world that generally seems to them futile and loveless,—a world in which they are impelled to ask Stephen Spender's question,—

> Who live under the shadow of a war,
> What can I do that matters?

Authoritarian religion thrives when the young wish to submit; and does this not further explain the vogue of the European writers of what Wyndham Lewis called the "trough between the wars"? For, if these writers were anti-liberal, they were opposed to nothing that millions of the democratic young really treasured; and, if ours has been a negative time, is this not because "love was not flowing in it," as Mabel Dodge Luhan said of one epoch of her life? * Various critics have explained that where, as in many war novels, death is always imminent, there is small place for love, because it "creates an oblivion" that is improper for a man in war "whose existence depends on preserving a tight hold over himself." † How many repeat that there is no place in the world for love today,‡ for

---

* "Everything having its two-fold character, only the negative aspects were apparent to me, at that time, for love was not flowing in me."—Mabel Dodge Luhan, *European Experiences*.

Does not this well convey the note of the "trough between the wars"?

† E.g., John W. Aldridge, *After the Lost Generation*.

‡ E.g., Wilbourne, in Faulkner's *The Wild Palms*: "Love if you will. Because it can't last. There is no place for it in the world today . . . We have eliminated it. It took us a long time,

one reason because of the liaison between "the soldier
and the whore," as one of Dos Passos's characters says
of a world in which, in a sense, all men are soldiers,*—at a time of lowered vitality, moreover,
when fecundity, fertility, productiveness are unfashionable qualities, despised and suspect in a writer. No
age has ever looked so askance at creative exuberance
and abundance as the age whose motto has been Hemingway's "not too damned much," an age in which
vitality itself has been regarded as vulgar, as it was in
literary Germany after the first world war.† What else
could one expect in a world enfeebled by the loss of
blood, exhausted by the unparalleled catastrophes of
two planetary wars? How can the depleted like the
full-blooded? And how can those whose nerves are

but man is resourceful and limitless in inventing too, and so
we have got rid of love at last, just as we have got rid of Christ
. . . If Jesus returned today we would have to crucify him quick
in our own defence . . . If Venus returned she would be a soiled
man in a subway lavatory with a palm full of French post-cards."

* " 'I have a theory,' Scott was saying, 'about the soldier
and the whore . . . War and bad times is when they flower. In
good times they lie dormant in society like a worm in a cocoon.
The hot sun of war brings them out . . . Other kinds of people
in the world build cathedrals, raise families, make bread and
champagne, weave cloth and grow vegetables. The soldier and
the whore destroy. The soldier destroys life. The whore destroys love; they have deep affinity for one another."—John Dos
Passos, *Chosen Country*.

† According to Franz Schoenberner, in *Confessions of a European Intellectual*, in literary circles in Germany after the first
world war "inborn vitality" was regarded as a "vulgar trait."
If one possessed this vitality one had to conceal it. Is this not
markedly true, also, at present, in certain literary circles in
America and England?

spent like to be reminded of the vital, the spirited, the copious, the superabundant?

How natural that at such a time the cult of wit should have returned again, with the vogue of the metaphysical poets, as an "escape from feeling," the wit that T. E. Hulme desired, like John Crowe Ransom later, and that has played a large part in contemporary verse. The merciless deflation of sentiment, a characteristic of the post-war mind that accompanies this wish to escape from feeling, has been accompanied in turn by a sort of fragile cynicism that prolongs the nineteenth-century *fin de siècle*. Once it is assumed that there is nothing to be done about the world and that even religion can be taken as a branch of aesthetics, one can understand the mid-century fashion of Ronald Firbank, for one example, who has something at least in common with Evelyn Waugh. For in what way do his people, who are constantly "flirting with Rome," who enquire whether Mary Magdalen was "engaged" to John the Baptist,—that is, "until Salome broke it off,"—who send as wedding-presents Flemish crucifixes with ruby nails for the hands and feet, while they tint their own toes with blackberries to look like nymphs,—in what way do they differ from Waugh's "posh Catholics" who are said to be saved because they observe certain rites? In their Mayfair religiosity they are all alike. All are equally money-worshipping self-indulgent worldlings, just as their creators are grandchildren of *The Yellow Book* and the smart aesthetic piety of Beardsley and Wilde. How natural too has been the vogue of Rilke, the valetudinarian, whom one might almost call the invalid as hero, the hypersensitive cosmopolitan who lived in the shadow of death and seemed to reflect the glow of the sunset of Europe. There are many strains and tastes in the mind of any period, too many to be embraced in a formula or a phrase, but, like individuals, periods too, in times of lowered vitality, naturally gravitate to philosophies of pain and defeat. They are allured by the elegiac and by poets who express a sense of the brevity, the frailty, the precariousness of existence; and, while some in our day are attracted to the wit that makes no emotional demand upon them, others are drawn to the existential. Still others, to Kierkegaard or Kafka.

For who could express more completely, in their different ways, the feelings of the helpless individual, tormented by doubts, overwhelmed by the sense of powerlessness and loneliness that have been so common in the "silent generation"? The uneasy ambiguous Kierkegaard, all mystery, melancholy, contradiction, inevitably found his late audience in the world-war epoch, if only because he embraced despair, from which alone, he said, one could achieve any real awareness of the spirit. Kafka, at the same time, conveyed in his nightmarish novels and stories the bewilderment and the masochistic strivings of many of the young. His people, ingrown, perplexed, unhappy, like so many of the displaced persons of today who have lost their sense of belonging anywhere, represent also the millions in modern cities who feel impotent, inferior, thwarted and alone. For how many is K. in

*The Castle* a symbol when he vainly tries to meet the authorities who refuse him the right to play his true part in the world, or the hero of *The Trial*, who is charged by a venal mysterious court and does not know the nature of the charge. Or Karl Rossmann, in *America*, twice disinherited, first by his parents and then by an uncle, for whom the whole world is a concentration-camp and who encounters nothing but arbitrary power, false accusations, injustices and misunderstandings that are more maddening still? He is lost in the interior of a ship, amid endless passages and flights of stairs, bereft of his possessions in the darkness, and later in a great fortress-like house with corridors that lead nowhere, blank walls, locked doors and empty rooms. A homeless wanderer in a world of sinister dwellings and more sinister men who behave with as little rationality as people in a dream, he knows only persecution and only frustration, with a sense of the utter futility of human effort.

Now if one asks for the reasons of the vogue of Kafka's "trilogy of loneliness," does one not find them sufficiently in the world of our day, especially among the sensitive who are insecure, desperate, uprooted, and for whom this world is a nightmare of dark corridors and blind alleys? And, in fact, do not most contemporary tastes suggest that people read now for help in the solution of their problems, their predicaments and plights, rather than for the objective interest that readers in so-called normal times found in Shakespeare or Molière or Goethe or Dickens? Do they not read now to find the company that suffering loves in

sympathetic minds,—like Rimbaud, for instance,—who
share their own malaise or disgust with the world? If
they are drawn to Baudelaire,—with his "natural pleasure in demolition" and a feeling of the baseness of
men that equalled Flaubert's,—to invalids, *poètes
maudits* and psychopathic writers, is it not through
this kind of fellow-feeling? Just so the tortured mind
of the present reads into Herman Melville a towering
metaphysical riddle that reflects itself, as it discovers
in Dostoievsky the violently irrational world it knows
and the sense of impending catastrophe that hovers
about it.

In short, do not people nowadays read mainly for
aid in the quest for security, which has become the
general quest of our time in a world that has come to
seem as irremediably evil as the post-Roman European
world of the early Middle Ages? * Then, as now, after
so much violence and anarchy, to find a safe haven was
all men asked for, though the world seemed scarcely
more evil than it seems in the day of the atom-bomb,
nor did men seem wickeder than they seem to contemporary writers. For to how many does our century
seem "disgusting," as it seems to the author of *The*

* "Dr. Frederick May Eliot, veteran president of the American Unitarian Association, has his own estimate of the mood of
orthodox Protestantism today: 'Black reaction and black pessimism.' The doctrine being emphasized, said Dr. Eliot at a Unitarian meeting in Cincinnati, 'is one of absolute despair, which
sets up as the only possible escape from cosmic disaster abject
submission to deity, the unquestioned acceptance of religious
authoritarian creeds, and the futility of human effort.' "—*Time*,
May 19th, 1952.

*Seven-Storey Mountain,* just as the culture of our
world seems "rotten, spurious, empty . . . not worth the
dirt in Harlem's gutters." For how many, as for
Thomas Merton, there is no hope in politics,—"all
more or less iniquitous and corrupt,"—so that nothing
in this world can stand as "a surrogate for Heaven";
and do they not see even childhood as Graham Greene
sees it when he says, "Hell lay about them in their in-
fancy"? For Graham Greene, as for many another, human nature too is "not black and white, but black
and grey," and "perfect evil," as he puts it, walks the
world "where perfect good can never walk again." In
an age that remembers Saint Augustine and forgets
Saint Francis, in which D. H. Lawrence's "dark forces"
seem to have triumphed, how many can see only the
sins and stupidities of men, the "desperately wicked"
of Jeremiah, the "fickle" and "false" of Machiavelli
and, one might say, of Freud as well. For Freud too
finds men basically antisocial, and he confirms the
views of those who, like T. E. Hulme, revived for the
literary mind "original sin." And does this not take
one back to the mediæval man, who wished to be
saved from himself as well as from the world? For his
world also knew nothing but sin and trouble. Who,
then, can wonder at the quest for security that is so
general in our day,—security in what Auden calls
"Catholic unity," in a return to the womb, or in
Baudelaire's big-bosomed mistress-mother? Or even in
the cynical negation that gives one a kind of security
by freeing the mind alike from beliefs and doubts?
And who can be surprised by what Elizabeth Bowen

calls "the tendency of writers" today "to take refuge in the past"?

For what, in the contemporary mind, has become of the future? Speaking of himself and referring to the novelists whom he discusses in *After the Lost Generation,* John W. Aldridge says, regarding the second world war, "Somewhere along the way tomorrow had been lost." This was the meaning of Gertrude Stein's remark, "The future is not important any more," and one might ask how the future can be important when the present seems so devoid of hope. For many today "history has failed," as Nicholas Berdyaev said; "there is no such thing as historical progress, and the present is in no wise an improvement on the past,"—which leaves no place whatever for thoughts of a future. In fact, who would not prefer the past, or the chance of turning back to it, when one sees in the future not only "No More Parades" but the kind of regimented world, controlled by "Big Brother" and the "Thought Police," with which George Orwell filled our imagination?

What then could be more natural than the revival today of that certain "homesickness" for the Middle Ages which Berdyaev defends in *The End of Our Time,* when "night is upon us," as so many feel, and "nowhere . . . is solid earth felt underfoot"? Berdyaev continues: "Modern history is an enterprise which has come to grief,"—it is being "wound up" and "an unknown era is upon us"; and the new world must be "the world of the new Middle Ages," a return to a "superrationalism of the mediæval type." For what has been the undoing of man but the "humanist illusions," the belief that the divine is imminent in him, the faith in man and his autonomous forces that came in with the Renaissance and developed into rationalism, liberalism, democracy and so forth? Now "all the usual trends of thought and ways of living adopted by the most 'advanced' people and 'friends of progress' are decayed past hope and no longer have a meaning," and what one must call "reactionary" now is the wish *not* to go back to a day when this life was regarded merely as a preparation for another. "The Renaissance came to nothing, the Reformation came to nothing, the Enlightenment came to nothing; so did the Revolution inspired by the Enlightenment." The good, the fine, and the lovable things are to be found in Eternity alone, though one finds them also in the past that touched upon it.

That we are witnessing,—and for these reasons,— the "end of the Renaissance," together with the "end of the humanism which was its spiritual basis,"—this is the meaning of the shift of interest from sociology to eschatology that Evelyn Waugh has observed in literary circles. Is not Karl Barth,—like Kierkegaard, so dominant in literary minds of late,—equally concerned to abolish the post-Renaissance conception that "man in the inmost depths of his being is divine" which gave birth to the modern man's belief in himself? Barth's "word for the hour" is that man is as "radically bad" as the Reformers thought,—and as others are constrained to think in a time of world wars,—and that consequently all the secular hopes of the modern mind are vain, while "this world is a ruin and a wreck, soon to be ended." History for Barth is a "never-ending process that never gets to its goal" and forces "the cry for another world" out of the heart, while all that happens on this earth is an illusion or a maze,—a "cheat and disappointment," as T. S. Eliot puts it. But more influential even than Barth in the literary world has been T. E. Hulme, who also attacked the Renaissance root and branch because, as opposed to the mediæval view, it introduced the notion of perfection on the plane of human things. That there could be no progress nor any human perfectibility the mediæval Christian was convinced, and, rejecting the world as a sad vestibule that merely led to the world beyond, he regarded the wheel as a symbol of the futility of living. Hulme lashed out at Goethe's "stupidity" for denying that the human mind, which seemed to repeat itself endlessly, was travelling in a circle, saying, "No, it is not a circle, it is a spiral," because, as a child of the Renaissance, Goethe exulted in the world and men and believed that in a sense they were tending both forward and upward. But was Goethe "stupider" than Hulme, who gloried in being "inhuman" as much as he gloried in being "pessimistic"? The answer depends upon whether one prefers the Renaissance acceptance of life or the mediæval attitude of renunciation.

One might mention other minds that have shared this renunciatory attitude, minds that have greatly influenced contemporary writers, among them Unamuno, whose phrase "the tragic sense of life" might almost be the motto of our generation. This paradoxi-

cal thinker was also possessed by what he called a
"nostalgia for the Middle Ages," and it pleased him
that, "forced to traverse," as he put it, the Renaissance
and the Revolution, his country had never lost its
"mediæval soul." * And how natural it is that so many
should feel the attraction of that epoch in our evil
world full of evil men,—as they are driven to see their
own epoch and people,—whether they are attracted in
faith or in fancy, like Henry Adams and certain of the
French Symbolist poets. For it appears to be an im-
perative need of the human mind to cherish some
golden age for contemplation, and the Symbolist poets
created Utopias of the past because they saw nothing
on which they could build in the future. Was not
Henry Adams similarly drawn to the days of the knight
and the troubadour because he found his world drab
and disappointing, so that he even convinced himself
that the degradation of modern man was part of a
predestined progressive cosmic process? The waning
Middle Ages have inevitably possessed for all these
minds a charm that survives a knowledge of their

* The writings of Unamuno are a perfect illustration of what
"eschatology" really means. Saying that "man's greatest crime
is that of having been born," Unamuno despised the Gallic *joie
de vivre*, and, insisting that "life is a preparation for death," he
was only opposed to suicide because it was, as he said, a bad
preparation. He was carried away by the "cult of suffering" and
the bleeding exsanguinate Christs of Spain, he exulted in "the
smell of tragedy," and, when a foreigner said to him, "You
people have no real love of life, although you are tenacious of
it," he replied, "Perhaps." He added, "The fear that if we die,
we die utterly and altogether, makes us cling to life, and the
hope of living another life makes us hate this one."

brutality and darkness,* the charm of the Van Eycks
or of Joan of Arc or Villon's poems or the plastic art
that, as Huizinga says, "does not lament." Still more,
of the religious fervour and the mystic peace that accompany a total abstraction of the mind from the
griefs and the joys of this world and life and a total
concentration upon thoughts of another.

Moreover, one finds a kind of security in dwelling
on those times in which everyone had his place in an
ordered social system, in which men were permanently
rooted, as it were, in a structuralized cosmos, ordained
by God, and no one was obliged to bear the burden of
freedom. At the price of everything that has made
the history of the last five hundred years,—good or bad
as this may be,—one can possess, in imagination, by
embracing the dream of that epoch, one's part in a
serene and stable cosmic whole. And is it surprising
that so many are eager to embrace it when they long

* See, for example, Meyer's *Annals of Flanders,* under date
1379, quoted in Lea's *History of the Inquisition:* "It would be
impossible to describe the prevalence everywhere of perjuries,
blasphemies, adulteries, hatreds, quarrels, brawls, murders, rap-
ine, thievery, robbery, gambling, whoredom, debauchery, av-
arice, oppression of the poor, rape, drunkenness and similar
vices." In the territory of Ghent alone, within the space of ten
months, there occurred, says this chronicler, "no less than four-
teen hundred murders committed in the bagnios, brothels, gam-
bling-houses, taverns and similar places."

The author of *The Waning of the Middle Ages,* the Dutch
historian Huizinga, says (in *In the Shadow of Tomorrow*): "If
those elegiac natures which long to see them [the Middle Ages]
return could pass but an hour in the midst of them, they would
gasp to be back in modern air."

only for "Comfort, out of Security, by Conformity" *
or even for security by conformity without the comfort? There will always be others who prefer to take
their chances in this world and who can accept the
consequences of living in it fully. But E. M. Forster's
"two cheers for democracy" are even more than one
can expect from those who are less than half-hearted
about life or about men.

* "Red" in James Jones's *From Here to Eternity*.

# CHAPTER VI

## A PROPHET OF OUR DAY

"WE ARE LIVING in a demented world," the Dutch historian Huizinga says, and, what is more, he adds, "we know it," but there are not so many who also know, with him, that there is nothing for us "but to go forward." That there is a way back, and that we ought to follow this, millions believe and feel in our nightmare world, in which we wake up to the nightmare instead of leaving it behind when morning dispels our painful dreams. Besides those who preach some sort of return to the mediæval synthesis, others invoke a wise passivity, the kind of submissiveness that one finds in Santayana and that many regard as yielding to the will of God. Having "bruised their hands," as Yeats said, on the "limit" of human striving, "men have at last come to see the world as an object of contemplation, not as something to be remade"; while Aldous Huxley's *Brave New World* and Orwell's *Nineteen Eighty-Four* have discouraged many minds from looking forward. They have covered with odium the conception of Utopia, in which thinkers formerly had visions of human goals.

That there is "something" still "to be made of life on this planet,"—the faith of Bernard Berenson,—few seem to believe, and even Albert Schweitzer says that "faith in the spiritual progress of men has already become almost impossible for us." We must "force ourselves to it," Schweitzer adds, we must "will" it "with the courage of desperation," for he would agree with Lewis Mumford that not since the century of the Black Death has the outlook for humanity been so dismal. Lewis Mumford also knows that our civilization is in danger of collapsing, he has shared all the nightmares of our time, he has heard all the prophets of doom from Burckhardt to Spengler and Henry Adams and he knows there can be no flight if the last wrath comes. He cannot share the old liberal belief that education will save the world because he is aware of the evils that elude education, the animal loyalties, the emotional drives, the outrageous irrational surges that the first world war brought into action. These tendencies, long hidden from the popular view, have nullified for Mumford the immature wishful utopianism of less conscious ages, and he has attacked the pragmatic liberal's "incurable optimism," that "wrinkled smile" left over from a sanguine past. Subscribing to the tragic view "in which the ultimate certainty of death counts at every moment in one's actions and plans for living," sceptical of all fair-weather philosophies, Lewis Mumford speaks, nevertheless,—no one speaks more, in fact,—of the "promise of our age." For our world, "endangered by its paranoia," is still, he says in *The Conduct of Life,* potentially exuberant, full, whole and balanced, and the most generous dreams of the past, practical necessaries

now, are only awaiting, to be realized, the "recovery
of purpose." Years ago Mumford wrote, "It is better
to face chaos courageously than to cherish the dream
of returning to an outworn synthesis," and he had his
word in *The Condition of Man* for the existentialists
for whom the world is meaningless, absurd and empty.
"The true answer to a meaningless existence," he said,
"is to conceive a pattern of life that possesses meaning
and purpose"; and one who has read him from first to
last becomes aware that the word "renewal" is the key-
word in all his thinking. Unwilling, like Schweitzer, to
admit defeat, although reason may say that the game is
up, Mumford repeats that "the renewal of life" is "the
burden and challenge of our time," a theme about
which, in his various books, he has a thousand things
to say that are wise, provocative, concrete, relevant and
stirring. He is possessed by a vital sense of the impetus
that flows through nature and man, insurgent, forever
expectant and forward-moving, and in terms of our
moment he carries on, like no one else living in America today, the tradition of Emerson, Whitman and
William James.

Mumford first became widely known as a critic in
the field of architecture,—a field in which he continues
to be eminent and active,—although it was evident
from the beginning that all his ideas and activities
sprang from a central philosophy, root and purpose.
What this was could have been divined in *The Story
of Utopias,* his earliest book, published in 1922, a book
that was derived from what might be called the Anglo-
American prophetic tradition of which Mumford

remains a prime representative today. This book dis-
cussed the various Utopias of which Anatole France
said that, without them, "man would still live in
caves, miserable and naked,"—since they are experi-
mental forecasts of a better future,—and he there distinguished between the "aimless utopia of escape" and
the "purposive utopia of reconstruction." Concerned
already with the recovery of purpose and the renewal
of life, he showed that, while "nowhere may be an
imaginary country . . . news from nowhere is real
news," answering the common objection to Utopia,
that it exists on paper only, by observing that the same
can be said of an architect's plans. As houses are none
the worse for these, so is society none the worse for
having its rational possibilities outlined in advance,
and thirty years ago he said what he repeated in *The
Conduct of Life,* "All challenges to animal lethargy . . .
begin in a dream."

He might have added that everyone dreams of a life
that is better than the one he knows, and that his own
critics have their day-dreams too, but that, with Eliot
or with Henry Adams, their dreams are nostalgic and
concerned with the past, a *terminus a quo* instead of a
*terminus ad quem.* And in what respect is Henry
Adams's thirteenth century or Eliot's mediæval Um-
bria, in which priests were never gross, any less unreal-
istic than William Morris's vision of a world of sanity,
good will, tolerance, grace and beauty? Mumford has
preferred the kind of dream that acts as an incentive
to the kind that rather puts the will to sleep, but he is
no less aware than his critics of the evil that exists in

man, nor has he ever been more materialistic. That "real life is . . . dogged forever by radical evil" and that evil has a positive role to play in life, he was to explain at length in *Faith for Living*, and no one has ever had more contempt for the "cog-and-wheel" Utopias that have coupled the salvation of men with the improvement of the machine. With no more respect than Dickens had for "Mudfog" Associations "for the advancement of everything" that remains external, he detests "our sterile mechanistic culture," and his notion of a reconstructed world implied already in his first book a "new set of habits" and a "fresh scale of values."

Mumford's developing ideas have followed a consistent line from the outward to the inward aspects of civilization, first the city and the machine, to which he has devoted two large books, the physical body of society, then the soul. Meanwhile, *Technics and Civilization* and *The Culture of Cities* were accompanied by *City Development, Sticks and Stones* and other studies of architecture and urban planning, in all of which he pursued the prophetic tradition of Morris and Ruskin and the great town-planner Sir Patrick Geddes. A professed disciple of the versatile Geddes and his "Outlook Tower" in Edinburgh, Mumford shared Ruskin's view that architecture has a social and ethical as well as a technical side, regarding it as more than a matter of building, or even of beautiful building, and as touching on all the major human interests. Beginning with the individual building, it led one on to the community design, while all that really mattered in it was that which "avails for life," a phrase in which Ruskin anticipated Mumford. For Mumford this explained the fact that there is so much beauty, as he said in *Sticks and Stones,* in an old New England village, and so little in our modern towns, beyond mere picturesqueness, because our modern architecture is so largely based on false ideas, Veblen's "conspicuous waste" or the "pillage of the past." Following Louis Sullivan's belief that "form follows function,"—in the words of the old Boston sculptor Horatio Greenough, —Mumford scorned the rank materialism of duplicating old forms because they please the eye. That these forms are necessarily empty without the life that filled them once, that there can be no such thing as a modern Tudor dwelling, Mumford regarded as only a part of the larger fact that "people, manners, feelings and architectural forms all go together." As "the aim of every generation must be to remodel," as he also observed, the "inner" and the outer world at once, what could be said for the contemporary taste for "twentieth-century kitchens, eighteenth-century dining-rooms and sixteenth-century studies"? An active taste "must show its respect for the past by leaving it where it belongs," he remarked in the brilliant essay *American Taste,* in which he declared once more his preference for the new architecture that is "clean . . . humane . . . friendly . . . adapted to every human need."

In his architectural essays and studies, Mumford has paid eloquent homage to the builders who have grappled with the realities of the American scene, endeavouring to humanize, while fully accepting, the forces of their place and time and turning them, raw as they were, to aesthetic ends. He has presented H. H. Richardson, Louis Sullivan and Frank Lloyd Wright as creators of new cultural forms in a world of adapters, a world in which plagiarism was, in fact, an emblem of reputability while they drew lessons from the world about them. They saw that factories and railway stations, office-buildings and waterworks, previously turned over to contractors and engineers who had no concern for art or beauty,—important elements of the modern scene,—afforded, as Mumford put it, the starting-point for a new architecture. This would belong to its own day, growing out of current needs, like all the valuable architectural examples of the past, and it was Richardson's vision of this that made him the first, Mumford said, to face the totality of modern living. Confronted with the problems of small-town libraries and suburban railway stations, he devised for them entirely new types of structure, analyzing the unprecedented functions to be fulfilled by them and creating forms with a corresponding logic and shape. "It was in the design, indeed, of new types of building that Richardson discovered his own sources of original design," Mumford wrote in *The South in Architecture*. Some of Mumford's finest expository writing is to be found in this series of lectures and in other studies of architectural subjects, the superb account, for one example, of Thomas Jefferson as an architect, with passages on the work of Richardson and Frank Lloyd Wright. One is not likely to forget Mumford's descrip-

tion of the shingled houses that Richardson made parts
of the New England landscape with his sage greens,
weathered browns and autumnal reds, resuming in the
colours he introduced the theme of the sumac and the
red oak, the butternut, the lichened rock, the sweet
fern and the pine tree. Rare are the critics of any sort
who could have the imagination to see how far
Richardson's country-houses belonged to the summer
landscape of their region, as the white farmhouse belonged to the snowy winter scene, or who could appreciate the genius of Wright in evolving architectural
forms that identify his houses with the settings of their
various regions. For the rest, in *The Brown Decades*
Mumford relates how three Chicago architects widened and modified the tradition that Richardson began until it became one of the main pillars of modern
architecture throughout the world.

In the course of these essays Lewis Mumford natural-
ized in many minds whole categories of American
artists who had been forgotten or whom people had
never previously thought of as artists, John Roebling
and his son, for instance, the creators of the Brooklyn
Bridge, a work of engineering that was also a delight
to the eye. Mumford called this a "poem of granite
and steel . . . one of those grand native works of art
that Whitman had demanded of the sayers and delv-
ers," a work that had been recognized earlier in the
same degree only by the admirable critic Montgomery
Schuyler. Another man whom Mumford called "one of
the great artists of the nineteenth century" was Frederick Law Olmsted, not forgotten, but scarcely signal-

ized before in quite this way, and then there was Eads of the St. Louis bridge and Schuyler whose *American Architecture* Mumford brought forward again as a neglected landmark. Another of these men was George P. Marsh, the old Vermont conservationist, the first to see how Americans were destroying their landscape, befouling and bedevilling the earth they lived on, while he outlined a course of action for saving the land; but most of all Mumford brought into common discourse the names of the eminent architects of whom Americans knew little. He taught his readers for the first time to look at their churches and public buildings, their banks, dams, factories and jails as works of art, or to ask why they could not be so described, for it had seldom occurred to Americans that building in America was connected with art as everyone knew it had been in European countries. American building was a joke in this country, where people spoke of the "Victorian Cathartic," or at best of the "Tubercular" or the "Cataleptic" style, and Mumford established in countless minds the names not only of the great builders but of the distinguished buildings which they had created. He showed how John Root's Monadnock Building in Chicago had influenced some of the new German architects, and he made Richardson's Marshall Field Building and Louis Sullivan's Auditorium as familiar names in the history of American art as Ryder's "Jonah and the Whale" or Whistler's "White Girl." He even pointed out the merits of the indigenous brick tradition of which excellent examples were to be found all over the South, a tradition that he said had never been appraised or examined, though its ornamentation was often conspicuously good, and he noted the beautiful High Bridge on the outskirts of New York that had carried the Croton water into the city. In these ways he widened the whole popular conception of what art is, on native grounds, together with the range and the nature of American artists.

In all this Mumford was playing his part in a widespread movement of the time, the recovery of the American past and its forgotten treasures, especially the work of the two generations immediately behind his own of which so many traces had been lost already. Through all the dun colours of the "brown decades,"—the theme and the title of one of his books,—the creative minds gleamed for his imagination, vivid, complex, harmonious, whether enriching or contradicting the sober prevalent colours that were so well known. He was a pioneer explorer of this obscure formative period in architecture, engineering, landscape design and painting, the age of Eakins, Homer and Ryder, as of Richardson, Olmsted, Roebling and Root, during which Herman Melville lived, obscurest of them all. Mumford was a pioneer in exploring the mind of Melville, too, before this became the subject of a five-foot shelf.

Thus Mumford shared in the effort of others to awaken our sense of the country's achievements. But he had for this a special and personal reason,—his faith in social as well as individual "renewal." He was deeply concerned for what he called, in *Faith for Living,* a "loving awareness of one's environment,"—which involved an awareness of its resources, in architecture, painting, literature, thought,—and a feeling that we "must concentrate our loyalties before we can expand them." Detesting what he called the "insolent fictions" of national sovereignty and isolation in a world in which "nothing less than the earth itself" is a "big enough place for any community to live in," he was convinced that patriotism was a "universal attribute of normal people . . . an indelible reality . . . grounded in space and time." Made up of common experiences and sights, places, ways and tools, it was founded on the actual soil and landscape of a region; and the region,—or the land,—with the family and the self were the three areas in which Mumford looked for his renewal. He said these three areas, which had always been life-sustaining, must always be central in plans for a new order, the family, the renewal of which was the theme of many of his essays, the self whose renewal was the theme of *The Conduct of Life*. Meanwhile, his concern for the renewal of the region was marked in his studies of city-planning, his reports on London, Honolulu and the Northwest, in which urban and regional renewal were considered together, all of them based on the understanding that metropolitanism it-self had already ceased to stand for progress. While Mumford always had at heart the development of his own native city, with a special feeling for characters connected with New York,—Walt Whitman, Herman Melville, Alfred Stieglitz,—he felt that great cities were "feral" rather than humane, like the wilderness which they had only imperfectly replaced; and the reader of his *Green Memories* knows how deeply planted his roots are in a region that is not too remote from Thoreau's Concord. That Americans are still the "nation of villagers" which Bernard Shaw ridiculed once is a fact that Lewis Mumford peculiarly delights in, and he looks to a "nation of neighbours and families" to "displace the economy of paper profits, paper joys and paper wealth."

When one speaks of the Concord of a century ago, one strikes a note that Mumford recalls in his writings and personality again and again, for he has as much in common with Thoreau and Emerson as he has with Ruskin, Morris and Patrick Geddes. He is clearly a prophet, in other words, of the line they represented, in one fashion or another, alike in America and England, and naturally he has been misunderstood in an age of pressure-groups in which critics are so largely given to hunting in packs. A solitary thinker where others are gregarious, with "one taproot that goes down deep," like Willa Cather's old farmer Neighbour Rosicky, vaguely "big" in the popular mind but unplaceable and troublesome, he has gone his own stubborn, intractable, thorny way. Too much alone with his own thoughts to be easily approachable, he admires Thoreau's Spartan austerity and taste for hardship, for the "pains, abstentions, renunciations" that are perhaps as essential for human development, he says, as more positive nurture. With what contempt he speaks of a civilization whose ultimate blessings are comfort and the postponement of death,—along with the "ottomans, ranged with pillows to meet each cushion of flesh with a softer cushion" that have so largely characterized modern living. In book after book he has castigated the self-indulgence of American ways, the attempt to live by the pleasure-principle that marked the state of mind of the nineteen-twenties, when sexual facility and relaxation became an imaginary panacea, as he said in *The Condition of Man,* for the ills of life. At that time all the by-products and sublimations of sex, he adds,—devotion, loyalty, aesthetic transfiguration,—were stigmatized as futile escapes from life, so that heroism and love were alike disparaged; and he has insisted that the restoration of rational inhibitions and sacrifices is now one of the conditions of human survival. With all the scorn of the author of *Walden* for bodily safety and ease,—convinced as he is that hard and tragic days are in store for all the world for at least a generation,—he shares Emerson's feeling for domestic life and Emerson's faith in the will, his profound belief that men are of "tunable metal." He combines with this the moral force of William Lloyd Garrison's motto "I am in earnest and I will be heard." For Mumford has the moral force and the savage indignation of the prophets of the Old Testament, as of England and New England, a force that is no longer recognized in a day of pragmatic acceptance when the cheapest sophistication has been regarded as a value. This is the force that made him a great pamphleteer in his fiery attack on fascism, *Men Must Act.*

In consequence of all these traits, Mumford is an anachronism,—that is, he belongs to one of the for-

gotten types, though this happens to be one of the
great classic literary types that inevitably recur with
changes in the literary weather. At the moment the
public mind has been conditioned against this type,
so that people do not know how to classify Mumford,
and more shallow nonsense has been written about
him,—while more perceptive things have been left un-
said,—than about any other important living writer.
Readers boggle at his difficulty while they swallow the
work of poets who do not even wish to be understood;
yet Mumford is one of the few Americans who are
now helping to think for Europe as so many Europeans formerly thought for us. His writings are hon-
oured in several countries where cities have been
wrecked and there is an eager welcome for his plans
for renewal, and his name has been called a household
word in England. It is true that Mumford seems to be
at odds with the *zeitgeist,* for he disagrees with all the
great parties of the time, the pragmatists and the orthodox religious along with the Marxists; while, un-
assisted by any clique, he has the exuberance and the
productivity that are suspect in contemporary critical
circles. He is too strong meat for minds, accustomed
to preciosity, that are inured to the fatalism of our
sad time, minds of low vitality that resent this passion
of affirmation, this faith in the creative instinct and
the world that is emerging. No doubt they resent as
well the positive tone of the prophet, in spite of Mumford's own belief that "the kingdom of absolutes is
not of this world" and that "life knows only partial
or momentary fulfilments." But there are many al-

ready for whom his powerful masculine mind has struck the rock, like Aaron, in our desert of stone and brought forth a stream of living water, somewhat as Emerson struck this rock five generations ago at a time when Americans were prepared for the conception of renewal. Our own might seem an unlikely time to suggest that "advance on chaos and the dark" which aroused so many minds in the eighteen-forties, minds that knew nothing of the paralyzing pessimism of the present. But who knows at what hour a new season may begin in our thinking? Our civilization, as Mumford observes, has not said its last word, and it may be prepared at any moment to enter upon the new world-culture of the future.

For Mumford man is "ready to depart on new missions," and he is himself in a strong position as a prophet of this world-culture because he is aware of the logs that block the path. He is not one of the bright young men who had never heard of sin until they discovered it in Reinhold Niebuhr's writings,— he has always known that the old-fashioned theologian, just because of his sense of sin, is more realistic than many supposedly enlightened moderns. The first world war unveiled for him the "whole nature of man," as it used to be called, in distinction from the rational side that had been taken for the whole, and he knew it included corruption, evil, the irrational desires that pragmatic liberals had never been disposed to admit. Even while princes were deposed, the demonic will-to-power remained, as craft remained when priest-craft was abolished. If Mumford stands by the

liberal faith, it is not because he does not know how
the pragmatic liberals have traduced it, unable as
they have been to see the "internal obstacles to external improvement" that he has so well described in
*Values for Survival.* Like the sun-dial, the pragmatic
liberals, Mumford said in *Faith for Living,* "cannot
tell time on a stormy day" because in their notion of
living there is nothing but sunshine, and so they could
never understand why the nineteenth "century of
progress" gave place to a half-century of savage re-
gression. He long since relinquished the optimism that
belonged to a constructive and expanding age,—
though this had been a healthy reaction against a
mouldering past,—together with the notion of progress
itself that grew out of an adolescent pride in the scientific conquest of nature and the invention of machines. For did not the rise of fascism prove that social
movement in a direction contrary to the direction of
world-civilization was not in the least unthinkable?
Mumford has never had any use for the nineteenth-
century dream of a liberation of mankind by mechan-
ical invention, for the values that count for him are
inner values; and he well knows that the planet on
which we live may become an extermination-camp at
any moment. On the subject of the atom-bomb he has
written with the verve that he brought to the subject
of fascism in earlier essays, while, detesting Spengler's
vulture-like mind, "gloating over the dead-food" of
culture-cycles, he knows that our civilization has been
disintegrating. None of the pessimists, in short, are
more aware than Mumford of all the negations of our

time and all the *buts,*—the qualifications that hedge modern affirmations,—and yet he has never for a moment lost that faith in the human potential which has marked all the major American leaders and thinkers.

This is the animating faith that has made his great tetralogy one of the imposing literary structures of the time,—*Technics and Civilization, The Culture of Cities, The Condition of Man, The Conduct of Life,* which project a new "open synthesis" or design for living. As Mumford says in one of these books, "If society is paralyzed today, it is not for lack of means but for lack of purpose," the kind of purpose that his own mind has been maturing steadily since he wrote *The Story of Utopias* thirty years ago. Dealing in turn with the machine, the city, the group and the personal life, he has carried out Thoreau's idea of building castles in the air and then placing foundations under them. For, first projecting new purposes and goals, he has explored the chances of creating form and order in a civilization in which we ascribe to our thoughts and feelings a lower kind of reality than we ascribe to external and physical objects. The only actual goods for him are the "good states of mind" that Clive Bell characterizes in one of his essays, and the mark of the machine age has been the dehumanization of man and the notion that economic values should dominate all others. And what can be said for extending the range of machines without any regard for plans of social control? Or for the habit of producing goods whether they are needed or not and utilizing inventions whether or not they are useful? The object of

Mumford's own study of technics has been to distinguish and define the properties through which it can serve life, as well as the powers that should be curtailed when they defeat this end or exist merely to support an economic system.

For the rest, as with all important books, there are many ways of reading these, and *Technics and Civilization* and *The Culture of Cities* abound with brilliant annotations on history, cultural and social. One recalls the discussion, for instance, of the manner in which the invention of the clock changed the general direction of human interest from heaven to the world in which we live, for time-keeping passed into time-attending and time-accounting and the rationing of time, and as this took place Eternity ceased gradually to serve as the measure and the focus of human actions. One recalls too the discussion of the way in which toys have fostered inventions,—the helicopter and the gyroscope first existed as toys,—and the part that glass has played in our social and spiritual history alike, modifying the inner world and the outer together. For the glass that made possible the telescope and the microscope, along with mirrors, spectacles and windows, seriously affected, as Descartes bore witness, all sides of humanity's outlook on life and the world as conceived by the scientist, the philosopher and the artist. With all his own concern for the future, Mumford is entirely just to the past, to the charms and perfections, for instance, of the thirteenth-century city, so greatly superior in certain ways to those "junk-heaps of discarded styles,"—the fruits of "cultural ragpicking,"—modern cities. For these styles are cut off completely from the culture that had given them a rational meaning, while the thirteenth-century city was all of a piece. For Mumford history is a reservoir of the discoveries of mankind to be constantly tapped and reëxamined. There he has traced, incidentally, the origins and growth of the machine civilization that we know at present.

That the age of the machine is passing, however, Mumford is convinced, and he says we are witnessing the last great crisis of a power civilization that is based on a wholesale denial of human needs and values. This civilization has been heading for the virtual extinction of man in a kind of sophisticated barbarism without soul or purpose; but, while the age threatens world-wide catastrophe, it holds forth also, Mumford thinks, an unexampled promise and the chance of a fresh life-drama. A new world has already come into existence, as yet in fragments only, a new culture emerging from our chaos of ideologies and creeds, but this requires a rebirth of the positive values of life, for the inner world of man has withered and shrivelled. The twentieth century, as Mumford puts it, inherited a morality that was the unearned increment, in reality, of religion, so that, like most rentiers, men are now unable to support themselves by their own independent efforts in the sphere of morals. The main task of our time is therefore to restore the value of personality, debased by a sordid debunking, in order to turn the helpless puppets of a deterministic world,—in Mumford's phrase,—"into wakeful and willing creators." This calls for a culture of the personality, a larger field for imaginative design than the building of a skyscraper, bridge or ship.

In short, in the new age the person must have the preëminent place, reversing the dehumanization that marked the machine age, so that ethics and the arts will dominate politics and technics; and this is the theme of *The Conduct of Life,* in which Mumford sets forth the conditions that are requisite, as he sees it, for moral renewal. Multitudes have evidently lost that sense of the difference between right and wrong, between good and evil, that is necessary first for survival before it becomes a condition of renewal as well; and when, under the guise of scientific neutrality, Freud's unexamined devaluations and unexamined values are projected on patients, is it not time to revive the art of conduct? Without this, immature personalities, irrational or demoralized personalities, are as inevitable as weeds in an untended garden, and the relativism of our day, insisting that all goods are of equal value, expressing ephemeral impulses and local tastes, denies the possibility of principles and universal standards. Mumford makes many suggestions that one can take or leave,—the idea, for example, of withdrawal and rejection before one returns to society reconditioned, the ideas of detachment for self-examination, thinning one's activity, slowing one's responses, extending the depths of life by contracting its surface. He makes much also of the culture of the family,—in which life becomes precious again,—suggesting the keeping of family journals, psychological records and the like, recalling the Concord practice of the Bronson Alcotts.

All these counsels are germane at a moment that requires a moral tightening of the bit when the watchword, no longer revolution, is integration, when the time has come, in other words, to reverse Blake's axiom and say "Bless braces and damn relaxes." It is by no means a cloistered virtue that Mumford has in mind, the goodness that displaces all other values, for he regards it as the aim of ethics not to promote good conduct merely but to further a more significant and abundant existence. For him, life is a dramatic struggle, with a constant clash of impulses, a perpetual conflict of forces both without and within, in which evil has a role to play and comfort and safety, not absolute goods, are as capable of defeating life as uncertainty and hardship. Nor, although he does not associate it with authority or historic institutions, is Mumford unmindful of the *mysterium tremendum* of religion. For him the ultimate lesson of democracy is that each must take upon himself the burden that was once transferred to messiahs and dictators and that man's business is not so much the mere contemplation as the active creation of the divine.

At this point Mumford brings to mind the vision of William Ellery Channing, who looked upon human nature as a godhead in the making, while at a dozen other points, recalling Jefferson, Emerson, Thoreau, he continues the classical American humanistic tradition. He revives this also in his faith in the creative powers of men, their capacity to do again what they have done, to change, remould, improve all their creations, the confidence in the native impulses of men that characterized the Enlightenment from which the American tradition directly sprang. That history has justified this confidence, Mumford suggests in *The Condition of Man,* observing, for instance, that the permanent gains in political government have arisen in states that respected the intelligence and will of their people. Appearing in the age of revolutions, this faith delivered emancipated minds from the tired worldly wisdom that condoned inertia and injustice. In a word, it released the actions that vindicate it; and this is the historic American faith that Mumford restates in terms of his own in a day of small hedonisms and small regressions.

# CHAPTER VII

## WRITERS AND THE FUTURE

WHAT DO WE FIND when we approach the contemporary novel? To return to John W. Aldridge, the author of *After the Lost Generation,* he says, referring to the novelists of the last few years, that they have inherited a world not only "without values" but without "a belief in the dignity and goodness of man . . . The sense of man's tragic yearnings, his endless struggles to attain the perfection of a god has been bred, analyzed and frozen out of them and replaced by a dazed contempt for his corruption and folly." That, along with a "stable order of values," a "basic belief in the goodness of man" is requisite for the performance of the novelist's function, Mr. Aldridge suggests again and again, agreeing with other American writers who have the well-being of their craft at heart, among them James A. Michener and Arthur Miller. For has not the author of *The Death of a Salesman* much the same point in mind when he says that many writers today are "mere chroniclers of disaster,"—instead of being "true tragedians,"—through "a cynical lack of faith that life has meaning"?—while Mr. Michener, assuming this is so, clearly asserts the positive note which the others find so generally absent now. "I find myself more deeply committed than ever," Mr. Michener says, "to the capacities for good in the average human being, and I believe that men trained in liberal thought will continue to be the instruments of triumph."

Now, whether or not these three men are eminent as writers, and whether or not they have otherwise anything in common, they seem to me to agree in stating a need of the moment in literature to which Lewis Mumford's American philosophy responds. Not that this is merely an American need or that Mumford is the only thinker to rebuke the "treason of the intellectuals" of our day,—which Toynbee calls their "cynical loss of faith in the recently established principles, and a nerveless surrender of the recently won gains, of Liberalism." As for the need in question,—the need of a stable order of values, together with a faith in life and the goodness of man,—is not this felt universally and have we not recently seen it expressed also in France? * There, in a symposium of the youngest generation, various contributors comment on the writers of the present and what they depict,—man as a derelict being, without wonder, purpose or ideals, bathed in an atmosphere that is sinister, oppressive and black. These writers give youth, which has always had the sense of a better day to come, nothing whatever now to attach its hopes to, and, merely reflecting an actual world in which all beliefs have gone by the board, they convey no faith whatever in constant val-

* In the magazine *Hommes et Mondes,* June, 1951.

ues. This repeats, more or less, what Mr. Aldridge says, and what Mr. Michener implies, like Arthur Miller, in a day in which so many minds "pursue and contrive endings and death," as H. G. Wells observed in his last little book. Lewis Mumford has replied to this with his traditional American belief in the dignity of man and the idea of progress, which Toynbee in his way corroborates also, seeing in the tapestry of history a "developing design" and in man "the master of his destiny . . . at least in some respects." With their sense of renewal, of fresh beginnings, both challenge those who abandon the world as what Barth calls inevitably "a wreck and a ruin."

But is not this negativism natural enough at a time when so many agree with Paul Valéry that "Europe is finished," when so much of the world has been exhausted by war and so many men seem to have justified the old conception of *homo* as *homini lupus?* That an epoch has really reached its term explains that sense of the endings of things which has filled so many minds for so many years, not only the obsessive preoccupation with civilization in decay but the belief that literature and art are dying. As much as Proust's world in France, even Faulkner's American world is represented as dying of senescence, and, soon after George Moore observed that literature was moribund, Spengler foretold the death of all the arts. Similarly, Ortega y Gasset remarked that the novel had "entered its last phase." This is all symptomatic of what many have called the general debility of our time, in France, Germany, England, the whole of Europe, where we have seen on every hand a shrinkage of creative power, a paralysis of nerve, a waning of artistic impulse. When an English statesman said, at the outset of the first world war, "The lights are going out all over Europe," he expressed much more than a political or momentary fact, and the chief loss of our civilization is the loss of the belief in man's free will, with man's confidence in his own ability to restore and to create. The prodigious change that came over the world in the latter half of the nineteenth century, with the development of the machine and all it stood for, is nothing to the change that has taken place since Freudian analysis and Marxian determinism destroyed man's belief in himself as the maker of his fate. When Swinburne wrote "Glory to man in the highest, for man is the master of things," he stood at the culminating point of a long evolution that began with the Renaissance four centuries before; and for many minds fifty years of human failure and human thought have served to reverse the whole of this long evolution. They see man not as the master of things but as the victim of original sin, just as man saw himself in the Middle Ages; and what, in their view, have people to live for and return to?—only

> The stale food mouldering in the larder,
> The stale thoughts mouldering in their minds,
> Each unable to disguise his own meanness
> From himself, because it is known to the other.*

One could scarcely express better that sense of the

* T. S. Eliot, *The Cocktail Party.*

meaninglessness of life which hampers and arrests the
work of the novelist today, with that low view of human nature which has the same effect, if we are to
believe Messrs. Aldridge, Michener and Miller. Faulkner seems to agree with them, for did he not say in his
Stockholm speech that, unless they express the "old
universal truths" of "love and honour and pity and
pride and compassion," all stories are necessarily
"ephemeral and doomed"? Faulkner added that, lacking this sense of the goodness of man and the meaning
of life, the contemporary writer "labours under a
curse," writing of lust instead of love, defeats in which
nobody loses anything of value, and victories without
pity and without hope. It is obvious that Faulkner,
nevertheless, belies in his practice this point of view,
which undoubtedly represents all the great writings
of the past, generally expressing, himself, as a novelist,
the nihilistic attitude that has largely governed writers
for the last thirty years. When André Gide said,
"There is not one of Faulkner's characters who, properly speaking, has a soul," he had not encountered the
old Negro in *The Old Man,* the convict who rescued
the woman and child in the flood; and there may be
other characters of Faulkner with as clear a sense of
honour and a pride in their own responsibility. But
in general is not the Faulknerian man the "creature
deprived of potentiality" of whom even Sartre has
written with disapproval? And does not this man suggest the philosophy of the father in *The Sound and
the Fury* that "all men are just accumulations, dolls

stuffed with sawdust swept up from the trash heaps where all previous dolls had been thrown away"?

It is one of the paradoxes of our time that Faulkner could write as he does of life and still defend so eloquently on a famous occasion not only the "soul" of man but the "duty" of the writer to lift men's hearts by reminding them of their courage, their honour and their pride. This is not to be explained by another statement which he made many years ago when he said that he wrote *Sanctuary* solely to make money and invented "the most horrific tale" that he could imagine because he knew that this was the way to do it. The present vogue of crime stories suggests the vast popular appetite for anything that assumes or proves the viciousness of man, and one might almost say now that popular success and critical success hinge equally on a low view of the human condition. To advertise a novel now, whether for popular or critical readers, one has only to call it "tough, sensational, brutal,"—I am quoting from the first book-supplement that is close at hand; and what writer would receive any critical attention who *carried out* Faulkner's expressed belief that a writer's duty is to lift the heart of man? But is it to be supposed that Faulkner, like so many other good writers of the time, dwell mainly on human degradation and human perversion merely to court popular success or critical esteem, although fashion undoubtedly governs the mind of countless camp-followers in the highbrow world as well as in the lowbrow world that cares mainly for money? No, if there is any trait that marks good writers in our day

*honesty*

it is a kind of honesty that one might call savage, a fierce sincerity, the sort of horror of all "untruth or exaggeration" that Hemingway expressed in his first book. And this precludes any concession to the bitch-goddess. So we must look elsewhere for an explanation of the paradox, the self-contradictory position that Faulkner presents, the fact that an honest man of genius "says" one thing and "does" another, as many writers of our time are constrained to do. The explanation is simple enough, that, whatever the faith of a writer may be, whatever his conscious conception of his function and duty, he is, when he comes to create, at the mercy of his unconscious mind and can only produce what this prompts him to deliver. And the writer cannot create his own unconscious. This is created for him by the climate of his time, its prevailing spiritual currents and modes of feeling; and in our time the unconscious minds of writers prompt them to see mainly the negative aspects of life. They transcribe the images that appear before their inner eye and that rise up from their own hidden depths; and, like Martin Luther, they "can do no other."

So it is the unconscious of our time that we see in the work of the novelists, and how could this be anything but a devil's brew, of which the most obvious element is the catastrophic defeat of man,—once thought to be "noble in reason,"—in two world wars. Infinitely smaller Acts of God have turned the minds of writers, as the earthquake that destroyed Lisbon in 1755 led all the optimistic thinkers of that generation to ask how far they had been wrong in supposing that the world was ruled by a benevolent Creator. If an earthquake could so affect Kant, Voltaire and Hume, how deep must have been the wound in the collective unconscious inflicted by events that destroyed for so many the secular hopes of mankind together with their faith and trust in human beings. And why in living America as in "dying" Europe? Because the whole promise of American life, as people used to call it, had been staked on these secular hopes and this faith in men, so that the human failure which the world wars represented seemed even more catastrophic in America than elsewhere. Besides, in all their wars the American armies had counted on winning, if not in the first battle, in the first campaign, and they had not only never been beaten but they knew nothing of the kind of wars in which, as we see now, the winner "takes nothing." It was as true in Korea as it had been in 1776, or in 1861, or in 1917, that they felt they had only to shout "The Yanks are coming" for the walls of all the Jerichos to fall down before them. They knew nothing of cold wars, or of stalemates, or the art of patience. No one has properly analyzed the direct connection between events and the states of mind and feeling of writers and thinkers; but defeat and frustration can lower one's estimate of man as much as the mass-murders of Buchenwald and Dachau. For the rest, can one ignore the connection between the collapse of the German Reich and the Barthian philosophy that arose in the midst of the collapse? Or between Berdyaev's point of view and the fall of the

czarist regime, which so obviously justified Berdyaev
for reactionary minds?

There has never been an age that moved so swiftly
from summer into winter,—or from what appeared to
be summer,—as the age we have lived through, the
"century of the child," as Ellen Key called it in its
hopeful opening years, that turned into the century
of Moloch, the eater of children. But of course it was
not summer that our winter emerged from; and, so
far as the estimate of man is concerned, Mark Twain
had come to feel much like Faulkner that human beings were dolls stuffed with sawdust. Like the Behav-
iorists, he saw man as a machine, or even as the "bad
monkey" of so many men of science, and it was only
a step from this to Mencken's man, "brother to the
lowly ass," the "king dupe of the cosmos," the "yokel
par excellence," the "booby." Nor was there any room
for Melville's or Walt Whitman's men, those "noble
and sparkling" creatures, the "kingly commons," in
the bleak world of Henry Adams or the worlds of
Marx and Freud that have largely shaped the modern
imagination. What is left to "sparkle" in the psychic
fragments of the decrystallized man that alone survive
analysis too often, while all that is "noble" is reduced
to discreditable causes, as that the feeling for justice
springs from envy? How many other influences, the
candid camera, the gossip column, the work of the
debunkers dismantling the hero, adding point by
point to the denigration of man, have contributed to
the devil's brew of the modern unconscious. "You
can't build a marble temple out of a mixture of mud

and manure," Larry says in O'Neill's *The Iceman Cometh,* nor can tragedy really be tragedy when the mixture of mud and manure is all that writers are able to make of man. For tragedy depends on a sense of the mind's "possible greatness," as Coleridge remarked in *Satyrane's Letters,* while "we can no longer tell tales of the fall of noble men because we no longer believe that noble men exist." *

These are a few of the elements that have gone to form what might be seen as a sort of "scorched earth" policy in contemporary letters, a continuation of the nihilism or the "great labour of destruction and negation" which the Dadaists believed they were obliged to perform. That this is not a policy but the result of a state of mind, springing from the general unconscious, which dictates to writers, one sees not only in the paradox of Faulkner, "saying" one thing and "doing" another, but in similar ambiguities in Hemingway, Dos Passos and others. The novelists of their generation, who created a pattern for younger men, were unable to see active goodness in developed human beings, or, rather, they were scarcely able to see developed types at all, or anything but "irresponsible criminals," as Edith Wharton put it.† They saw Amer-

---

* Joseph Wood Krutch, *The Modern Temper.*

† "The poor novelists who were my contemporaries (in English-speaking countries) had to fight hard for the right to turn the wooden dolls about which they were expected to make believe into struggling suffering human beings; but we have been avenged, and more than avenged, not only by life but by the novelists, and I hope the latter will see before long that it is as hard to get dramatic interest out of a mob of irresponsible

ica as virtually peopled with "shady characters," Auden
has said,* "heroes without honour" whose only virtue was "a stoic endurance of pain and disaster," "irresponsible victims" who were never "responsible
agents." Man, in their novels generally, Auden added,
was "the absolute victim of circumstances and inca-
pable of choice." There were few children who stood
for hope, few wise old characters in their books, and
where could one find in any of them a man of their
own people who evoked the admiration that Hemingway could feel for a horse? Only in Spanish peasants
could Hemingway see "nobility," as Faulkner could
see it in a Negro, but in terms of ordinary human life
did they ever lift the heart or convey a sense of pride
or compassion or honour? And did not Dos Passos
seem half-hearted when, in his later work, he defended
marital integrity, affection for the country, and all the
"eternal necessary human values" that Scott Fitzgerald
proclaimed,—and omitted from his stories? Whatever
the conscious intention of any of these writers might
have been, or their wish to present the positive values
of life, the devil's brew of the unconscious of their
time proved to be too much for them and kept them
from realizing Faulkner's conception of their "duty."
Their minds were conditioned against the sort of
broadly human view of life that one found in certain

criminals as out of the Puritan marionettes who formed our
stock-in-trade. Authentic human nature lies somewhere between
the two, and is always there for a new great novelist to redis-
cover."—Edith Wharton, *A Backward Glance.*

* In *Harper's Magazine,* July, 1948.

of the writers of the previous generation, who saw, as
Willa Cather saw, or Ellen Glasgow, or Sinclair Lewis,
the goodness that often predominates in the nature
of men. For, whatever their perception of goodness
might be, it seemed only to *float* in their minds, as if
they were scarcely able to believe it was real. Or as if
they scarcely cared whether it was real or not. In much
of Faulkner, as in Erskine Caldwell, one never knows
whether the author feels any compassion for his victims or any real wish that the characters and conditions of these victims might be other than they are.
The author seems often to be merely gloating over the
squalor that he presents, as if he regarded all values
as equally indifferent.

Plainly, then, the younger writers have inherited
what Mr. Aldridge calls their lack of a belief in values
and the dignity of man; and are they not quite generally now "selling human nature short," as Don M.
Wolfe says in his preface to *American Vanguard?* They
are "looking away . . . from the noble figure who em-
bodies despite his weaknesses what William Faulkner
called 'the old truths,'" presenting, says Mr. Wolfe,
an image of human nature "so narrow as to be a hor-
rible caricature." * This writer cites James Jones, William Styron and Norman Mailer as among those who
ignore the "superior man or woman," but of how
many others he might have spoken whose range of
types is virtually confined to the "shady" and "irresponsible" characters to whom Auden has referred?

* Don M. Wolfe, *American Vanguard*, 1952.

Hell-bent for destruction, their younger people are generally corrupt, often depraved, alcoholics, homosexuals, morons and incestuous children, like the monkeys, quacks, crooks and whores of Evelyn Waugh's novels that seem to embody a hatred of humankind. Their authors appear to be echoing the remark of Flaubert that life is like "the odour of bad cooking through a venthole"; while, concentrating as they do on sex, they omit most of the overtones that alone make sex significant to the intelligent reader.

These are the "mere chroniclers of disaster" of whom Arthur Miller speaks and who are deeply concerned with virtuosity only, the technical proficiency which evidently means so much to them and which they often develop with a masterly adroitness. And is this not worthy of respect? Of course it is so; though when, aside from the way of saying it, one considers what is said, then one is driven to question its ultimate value. How can such work stand up beside the work of the old Russian writers which always embodied in fiction a regenerative impulse? When Chekhov said that the "good" writers are always "going toward something and are summoning you towards it, too," so that you feel in their work, "besides life as it is, the life that ought to be, which captivates you,"—when he said this he was speaking as much in the line of Faulkner's Stockholm speech as in the line of Turgenev and Dostoievsky. For was this not Turgenev's note in *Memoirs of a Sportsman?*—as it was Dostoievsky's note when he recognized the goodness in so many of the imprisoned criminals of *The House of the*

*Dead.* Where can one find in a Russian writer the absolute night of American writers for whom so many
human creatures are irretrievably damned? Not even
among the thieves, down-and-outs and suicidal wrecks
in the bunkhouse in Gorky's *A Lodging for the Night.*
All living things in that poisonous air might have
been expected to wither and die; yet there one finds
the old pilgrim Luka whom grief and disappointment
have never robbed of his faith in the goodness of mankind. Luka believes that every man, however degraded,
can be reached and that reasons exist for respecting
the humblest and the lowest; for one never knows
from which one "strength is to be born." Why do men
live? Luka asks. Only to give birth to strength; and
who can tell what anyone may prove to have in him?

To arouse in man "faith in himself," Maxim Gorky's
object, is not the aim of the American writers I have
mentioned, for the unconscious of their time commits
them to believe that man is the helpless victim of his
own tendency to evil. It is true that we have other
writers, novelists and playwrights,—many, in fact,—
who present the everyday heroisms of quite ordinary
people; and, moreover, while some have sincerely
come to believe in the doctrine of original sin, there
are more for whom this is a phrase and theology a
game. Has not Auden spoken, in a published note, of
the "constant tendency of the spiritual life to degen-
erate into an aesthetic performance," a tendency that
has been encouraged in literary circles by the stress
that is laid on the intellectual content of religion?
How many who love to think of tradition in connec-

tion with religion and associate themselves with religion because of its tradition would have shuddered at the sight of the Twelve Apostles and shivered in the dawn of a faith that had not yet established a tradition! Are these not making, in some sort, a game of religion?—like T. E. Hulme when he said that he "swallowed, for the sake of the dogma" of original sin, "God, Freedom and Immortality . . . quite secondary matters." How many critics nowadays prefer one theological view to another because, as they say frankly, they find it "more amusing," forgetting that, measured from this point of view, Edward Lear's *Book of Nonsense* is more amusing than either. So there are twenty who find it amusing to think of man as "fallen" to one who *believes* man has fallen, and believes it with regret, while for others "evil" and "sin" are words which they use for aesthetic effect and even for decorative purposes, as one might put it. They play with the "desperate wickedness" of Jeremiah as if this were a theme for a jingle or a tableau or a ballet, while any precocious child can talk of the "tragic view of life" as the infant Pope lisp'd in numbers, for the numbers came. The conception that man is base and life is nasty has become in our generation as automatic as the opposite notion was fifty years ago, and pessimism is obligatory now as optimism once was and as the "happy ending" used to be. Even Hollywood has gone over to the unhappy ending.

There are reasons enough for the misery that weighs upon the modern mind; and can we not see in the play-element in contemporary writing at least in part an attempt to escape from this? When reality seems too formidable to be dealt with directly, it is natural for writers to retire into a world of their own, poets into private hieroglyphics, critics into puzzle games and novelists into games with stylized puppets. And why should there not be a literature in which metaphysics, method and form supplant the human element as well as the "message"? There is no reason why novelists and poets should not have this kind of art so long as they are willing to accept two provisos,— that they cannot both keep *and* spurn the common reader and that for their purpose they cannot cite Faulkner. For the human element is paramount in Faulkner's position, as it is paramount with those who wish to represent man and life but see life *only* as nasty and man *only* as vile. But are not these novelists actually killing the novel, the modern novel that an English critic has recently called "the withered branch" because it so lacks significant human content? With its presented agonies of maladjustment, frustration, suspense, all sufficiently true to the world we know, it shows only "the stale food in the larder" of life without the fresh yeast that also exists,—the "irresponsible victims," never the "responsible agents." Why was the "renaissance" of the nineteen-twenties not renewed? Why, having flourished so vigorously, has it steadily declined, as sympathetic critics of the novel have so generally remarked? And have not many novel-readers turned to biographies instead because these are *obliged* to deal with significant people? One might call this a judgment on "these soul-dissolving novels, melting down the very sinews of our pride," as one of our novelists, Isabel Bolton, calls them,— stories of "raw-head and bloody bones" that awe the human mind, in Thomas Jefferson's phrase, "to a distrust of its own vision."

If negation and cynicism have had this effect on the novel, if a disbelief in values and the dignity of man have driven it more and more into a corner, is it not time to ask how far one can doubt the existence of values and whether mankind is as low as the novelists suppose? When Christ said, "Ye have Moses and the prophets, hear them," he might have been speaking for all peoples along with the Jews, for the ethical systems of all the great cultures are much alike in their view of the norms that follow from the nature of man and favour his growth. All the great moral codes agree on what is right and wrong; the ideals of most of the higher religions are the same, and regarding generosity, honesty, kindness, fortitude, patience and courage, the sages of all times and races are of one accord.* Is not love known to be better than hatred and charity

* "About the middle of the third century before Christ, Asoka, the Buddhist ruler of India, had carved on rocks and pillars at various points throughout his vast empire recommendations to practise certain virtues. These virtues will be found to be nearly or quite identical with those enumerated by Saint Paul as the fruits of religion: 'Love, joy, long-suffering, kindness, goodness, faith, mildness, self-control.' Chinese, again, who know the Confucian books—the main source of the humanism of the Far East —are struck at once by the substantial accord between these books and the *Ethics* of Aristotle, perhaps the most authoritative single document in the humanistic tradition of the Occident."— Irving Babbitt, *Spanish Character and Other Essays.*

better than revenge, are not hypocrisy and cowardice by everyone condemned, and is not civilization based on truth-telling, which might be called a physical fact inasmuch as we have a machine that detects a lie? Does anyone fail to applaud Huck Finn when he decides to save Nigger Jim, although he thinks he is damning his own soul thereby, for he is certain that if he abets the old slave's flight he will be condemned to hell as a breaker of the law? Does not everyone applaud the young man who, in *The Devil's Disciple,* assumes on the scaffold the place of a man he dislikes?—as one applauds Shaw's Androcles who cannot go back on his faith although he expects, in consequence, to be thrown to the lions. Who fails to respond to the theme of *The Glass Menagerie* of Tennessee Williams that "purity of heart is the one success worth having"?—as most of us share Voltaire's respect for tolerance and good temper and regard them as indispensable to civilization. So how, in the face of this general agreement, can one doubt the existence of values? And how can one doubt that these values are deeply rooted in the general mind, for all its indiscipline, grossness and worship of success?

For the rest, is man as inevitably base as the novelists seem to think he is, the "fallen creature with a natural bias to do evil," the grasshopper who is always looking for "dung to stick his nose in" that Mephistopheles characterized in *Faust?* What said the Lord to this "spirit who denies," who "finds nothing right on earth,"—and who might have been an American novelist of the moment?—that, although man is prone to err, still, through obscurest aspiration, he has "an instinct of the one true way." To say the least, are not men ambivalent? Their nature is not inalterable; there is no scientific evidence to support the assumption that the psyche comes into the world with an original stain; and, in fact, the "natural badness" of men is the same sort of presupposition as the "natural goodness" that so many repudiate now. Both are presuppositions, as Auden says in *The Intent of the Critic,* and perhaps in large measure temperamental, as one sees in the two characters in Galsworthy's novel *The Aristocrat* who stand for the division of minds that disturbs us now.* Or, at least, this *should* disturb us, considering how

* " 'Distrust of human nature—fear . . . You deny the right of the individual to judge, because you've no faith in the essential goodness of men; at heart you believe them bad. You give them no freedom, you allow them no consent, because you believe that their decisions would move downwards, and not upwards . . .

" 'But the world is not ruled by power, and the fear that power produces, as you think, it's ruled by love. Society is held together by the natural decency in men, by fellow-feeling. The democratic principle, which you despise, at root means nothing at all but that. Man left to himself is on the upward lay . . . A man knows unconsciously what he can and what he can't do without losing his self-respect. He sucks that knowledge in with every breath. Laws and authority are not the be-all and end-all, they are conveniences, machinery, conduit pipes, main roads. They're not of the structure of the building—they're only scaffolding.

" 'We are at the bed-rock,' cried Courtier. 'Your God is outside the world, mine within it.'

" 'And never the twain shall meet,' Miltown replied."—John Galsworthy, *The Aristocrat.*

much depends on our decision to take one side or the
other.* I assent myself to the positive side, for faith in
human goodness has meant so much for the advance
of men that I cannot abandon it lightly or in the
fashion of the moment. And can this goodness properly be called a "myth"?

That goodness abounds we all know, just as we
know what it is, in spite of what is often called the
"decay of moral values"; and we might be readier to
affirm the prevalence of goodness if we did not fear to
seem too easily pleased. There are great characters all
about, like Albert Schweitzer or the "Burma surgeon"
or Helen Keller or Andrew Furuseth, the Norwegian-
American leader of the Seamen's Union who lived for
the welfare of seamen throughout the world.† These
are the heroic types that expand the meaning and
value of life, and their qualities are as plentiful today
as in any other epoch, though the minds of writers are
conditioned against them and do not see these qualities in an age that, as Eliot says, "objects to the

* "The statement, 'Man is a fallen creature with a natural
bias to do evil' and the statement, 'Men are good by nature and
made bad by society' are both presuppositions, but it is not an
academic question to which one we give assent. If, as I do, you
assent to the first, your art and politics will be very different
from what they will be if you assent, like Rousseau and Whitman, to the second."—W. H. Auden, in *The Intent of the Critic*,
edited by Donald A. Stauffer.

† "They cannot put me in a room any smaller than I have
always lived in. They cannot give me food any simpler than I
have always had, and they cannot make me any lonelier than I
have always been. Let 'em come."—Furuseth's words when he
was told that he was to be arrested for so-called seditious speaking. Quoted in Jo Davidson's *Between Sittings*.

heroic." For the rest, no one defends today the "noble savage" of Rousseau's time, although anthropologists who have known the savage as a type have justified in part this implausible notion. Moreover, there is Schweitzer, who knows the primitives of the African forest, while he is eminent alike in judgment and in feeling, and who, though he does not range himself on the side of Rousseau's "idealization," ranges himself far less on the other side. What Schweitzer says is that, while Rousseau idealized the child of nature, there was truth, nevertheless, in his views about him, in his belief in the savage's possession of "high moral and rational capacities . . . No one must think," Schweitzer continues,* "that he has described the thought-world of the Negro when he has made a full list of all the superstitious ideas which he has taken over and the traditional legal rules of his tribe. They do not form his whole universe, although he is controlled by them. There lives within him a dim suspicion that a correct view of what is truly good must be attainable as a result of reflection,"—which understates, to say the least, what many anthropologists affirm and what Herman Melville said of the Marquesans.† There are, for

---

* *On the Edge of the Primeval Forest.*

† The Marquesans "seemed to be governed by that sort of tacit common-sense law which, say what they will of the inborn lawlessness of the human race, has its precepts graven on every breast. The grand principles of virtue and honour, however they may be distorted by arbitrary codes, are the same all the world over; and where these principles are concerned, the right or wrong of any action appears the same to the uncultivated as to the enlightened mind. It is to this indwelling, this universally

instance, the anthropologists whom Havelock Ellis cites in his essay *The Origin of War* and who say that "peace, not war, is the normal condition of the Australian tribes" and that "for the most part savages are gentlemen." It is true, no doubt, that much infantile sadism coexists in primitive people with their hospitality and kindness, enough perhaps to warrant Dr. Johnson's warning, "Don't cant in defence of savages," to Boswell. But can one forget that Rousseau's "noble savage" was drawn from the Jesuits' Relations of their dealings with the red men? So Sir Thomas More sketched his Utopia from Amerigo Vespucci's reports of America, where the Indians had given him the idea that all men might be free, and that government might rest on the consent of the governed, as Grotius's philosophy of international law was largely founded on other reports of the new world's primitive people. The example of the American Indians had convinced these travellers that international dealings might be based on mutual accommodation and on reason, and Grotius proceeded to establish international law on a fundamental faith in the goodness of men.

It seems odd enough that at this late day one can still debate the old Rousseauist presupposition which Auden rejects,—that men, "made bad by society," are "good by nature"; but are we not compelled to do so when many have revived the far more debatable notion of original sin? If we are concerned with the basic

diffused perception of what is just and noble, that the integrity of the Marquesans in their intercourse with each other is to be attributed."—Herman Melville, *Typee*.

man, what do the anthropologists say? Are they not closer to Rousseau than to St. Augustine or Calvin? *
And does not Ashley Montagu's *On Being Human* indicate that the "drives toward good" in man are as "biologically determined" as his "drives toward breathing"? That "the biological facts give a biological validation to the principle of coöperation, of love, in human life," this anthropologist seems conclusively to prove, as that men's "hostile" tendencies spring from the frustration of an innate need for love, and the response to love, on the part of the child. Even though all the surface evidence points in a contrary direction now, when "fission" is the word of the moment, the opposite of "fusion,"—whether with respect to physics or human affairs,—nevertheless, this writer shows that "fusion comes much closer to reflecting man's natural behaviour patterns . . . The view that the child is born egocentric, evil, in 'sin,' is widely held, and it is nothing more than the projection upon the child of our own conditioning in egocentricity, in evil, in 'sin,'" whereas the view that the child is born as an actively coöperating organism is a view supported by the facts. "Evil" states are "disharmonic, unviable, unstable and malfunctional states." They are the "unpleasant states" that a child necessarily avoids if its needs are adequately satisfied, this writer says,—it cannot then help

---

* E.g., Franz Boas when he speaks of "the suspicion long held by anthropologists that much of what we ascribe to human nature is no more than a reaction to the restraints put upon us by our civilization . . ."—Preface to Margaret Mead's *Coming of Age in Samoa.*

"being good,—that is, loving." For "all of man's natural inclinations are toward the development of goodness, toward the continuance of states of goodness and the discontinuance of unpleasant states."

Now if this were all merely asserted by a well-intentioned literary man no one would pay the least attention to it, but Ashley Montagu's affirmations are based on the sort of evidence that twentieth-century minds are conditioned to respect. When he says that "evolution itself is a process which favours coöperating rather than dis-operating groups," he refers to a wide range of biologists and psychologists who reverse the beliefs of the so-called Darwinians of the past. This is true also when he says that "all human beings want to be good . . . all human beings want to be happy," and "their biological drives are calculated to achieve these ends," while "there are certain values for human life which are not matters of opinion but which are biologically determined." These are the values,—are they not?— essential for the well-being of man and for the survival of the race as well, that have been called "universals" and are certainly "constants"; though people may talk as they will of the relativity of morals. In *The Proper Study of Mankind,* based largely on the Cross-Cultural Index,—a summary of the findings of anthropologists that has been compiled at Yale,—Stuart Chase enumerates these universals. They are the principles that men of all races hold in common, and they are founded upon the fact that any society would fall apart if people were not generally honest and solicitous for their children, if they did not, on the whole, maintain domestic stability and loyalty in friendship, if they did not in times of stress stand by others. Hume said that history's chief use was "only to discover the constant and universal principles of human nature," and anthropology accomplishes this by summing up these principles that have governed men from the jungle to the modern farm and city. What stands out from the record is not so much the differences as the profound similarities of societies and men, their general agreement in regard to values that are as constant as the needs they express and as universal, correspondingly, as these needs are also.

Is this not something to bear in mind when, as Stuart Chase says, "a time for revaluations and new concepts is at hand" and when he can add that "all generalizations and theories must be founded on these principles" which have governed the whole of mankind? Surely, this disqualifies all applications in the moral sphere of the relativism that denies the universal, just as it corroborates the virtual consensus of all the wise regarding the "eternally necessary human values." How did it happen that Joseph Wood Krutch was so drawn to Dr. Johnson, of whom he wrote a fine biography, when he had made such a point of telling us in *The Modern Temper* that nothing was more temporary and relative than moral values? Have not Dr. Johnson's name and fame endured so long solely because of the good sense which emanates from him and which, in spite of his tory intolerance, seems to confirm a feeling in ourselves that the most important things are universal and constant? Is not the perennial charm of Dr. Johnson a living confutation of *The Modern Temper?*—as one might go on to ask why the Greek and Roman classics have endured in a similar way for two thousand years? What is a classic, in point of fact, if it is not a proof of the permanent existence in men of that which *responds,*—of elements in the human mind that survive and transcend great stretches of time and bridge every difference of environment and race? What brings the book and the reader together can only be the presence in both of something constant that is also universal.

Then what shall we say of the novelists who see only the "corruption and folly" of men, and for whom society possesses no "order of values," except that all they write, while "true," is surely not "the truth," to quote Mahatma Gandhi in a well-known connection? Man has a will, as history shows, and the novelist also has a will,—for how without a will could he write novels?—and there is ample evidence that men have an inborn tendency to grow, to develop their potentialities, to expand, to be "normal." There are highly respected psychologists who agree with Dr. Johnson that "the worst man does more good than evil" and who say there is reason to believe that it is natural for men to strive not only for happiness but for truth and justice. Evidently, therefore, the novelists for whom nothing exists but the "low-down" are by no means presenting reality in its length and breadth; and, if negation and cynicism are destroying their art, is it not in their own interest to clarify their vision? But can they do this by willing it, conditioned as they are and poisoned beyond all question by the unconscious of their time, which has created their own unconscious and prompted their inner eye to see only the dark images of life that appear in their novels? Can they by means of their will rectify their vision, even if all the admonitions addressed to them bristle with "oughts" and "shoulds" and Faulkner says they "must" learn the old verities again? What is the force of so many imperatives when the spiritual climate of our time has effectively destroyed their belief in the freedom of the will and when passivity in every sense has been inculcated in them, with habits of pragmatic adaptation and pragmatic acceptance? "Joyce, Proust, Eliot and Virginia Woolf," said Stephen Spender in *World Within World,* "turned a hero or heroine into a passive spectator of a civilization falling into ruins." None of them ever conceived of a hero who *acted on* civilization, or even dreamed of so doing, to save it from ruin, any more than our novelists have conceived of a hero to whom it occurs for a moment that he can shape his own life for admirable ends. Their heroes have been virtually all like Hemingway's man whom "things are done to," seldom the man who *does,* as Wyndham Lewis put it,—for instance, Fitzgerald's Dick Diver who was "swallowed up like a gigolo" and "permitted" himself to be swallowed, his creator said. They are "fallen" men who have willingly fallen, passively following a way of life that inevitably leads to death, defeat or downfall, never choosing consciously between the evil and the good or apparently considering it possible to make this choice. And are they not expressions of the minds of their authors?

What then "must we do?" as Tolstoy asked, if writers cannot believe in the will, if they cannot see man as a "reservoir of possibilities" any longer, although, until they regain a sense that life and mankind have meaning and value, they can only add to the despair and the sickness of the time. Are we obliged merely to wait for the next great man of genius, who will turn the current for us, as assuredly he will?—for the present state of the literary mind cannot continue much longer in fiction, in poetry, in criticism, in any department. Writers in general have reached a sort of North Pole, an "icy aloofness from humanity," as Peter Viereck sees them; and, standing at absolute North as they do, whichever way they face, their next step can only be "toward the broad southlands of humanity." The great original writer of genius who will dominate the coming time is almost certainly destined to take this step; and will he not restore for us the notion of the author as Augmenter,—"he who augments" the territory of the City of Man? (As the generals who made conquests for Rome were called Augmenters.) The real augmentations are not additions of technique, such as the writers of the last generation yielded: they are additions of what Bernard Berenson calls "life-enhancement," heightening and intensifying our feeling for the human condition. The true augmenters are those who retrieve our confidence in man and in man's latent capacities and creative powers, appealing to his honour and good faith while relying upon his possession of these, an attitude that has worked wonders in education. Enemies of all that diminishes men and denigrates human existence, they are active promoters of the good and creators of beauty, that "corpse" for the contemporary mind which, in Paul Valéry's phrase, "crude excitement" has supplanted. But does not the "cult of beauty," as Ezra Pound once remarked, stand for the "art of cure," as the "art of diagnosis" is connected with the "cult of ugliness" which reigns at present and with the "diagnostic" writers who have had so long a run, among them Flaubert, Baudelaire, Corbière and Villon? * And if "beauty in art reminds one of what is worth while," if it is "hygiene, sun, air and sea," is it not something to think about in a time as sick as our time that has had so much diagnosis and so little cure?

For, if we accept this definition, virtually all our contemporary writing might be described as diagnostic; and does it require an act of will to think of this other kind of writing and even to fill our imagination with it? Although the literary rank and file always naturally take for granted the absoluteness and per-

* "As there are in medicine the art of diagnosis and the art of cure, so . . . in literature . . . are the cult of ugliness and the other, the cult of beauty.

"The cult of ugliness, Villon, Baudelaire, Corbière, Beardsley are diagnosis . . . Flaubert is diagnosis.

"The cult of beauty is the hygiene, it is sun, air, and the sea and the rain and the lake bathing . . . Beauty in art reminds one of what is worth while . . . You feel bucked up when you come on a swift moving thought in Plato, or on a fine line in a statue."—Ezra Pound, *Pavannes and Divisions*.

manence of the modes of any given present, these
modes are mutable, they are destined to change,
while the constant need remains to *re*humanize whatever is *de*humanized in life or in art. If this need is
obvious now, is it not obvious also that we must
break the habits of the recent past, following the advice of William James who said that if one acts a part
one presently develops the feelings that implement the
action? As *l'appétit vient en mangeant,* so the belief
in the will returns if one acts as if one had a will, and
health too has often been known to return when,
ignoring sickness and acting the part of health, one
finds oneself well. To rehumanize literature, meanwhile, the first step is to think better of man, to celebrate the grandeur of humanity and rejoice in its
nature, to repudiate the meanness of the minds that
love to dwell on the "stale thoughts" which are all
one with the "stale food mouldering in the larder."
We should elevate and honour men, proud of the great
things they have done since their anthropoid-forbears
climbed down from the jungle trees, since, discarding
their tails and fur and walking forth as human, they
looked before and after, knowing good from evil. The
honouring of men is the only reply to the degrading
of men that has accompanied the nihilism and regres-
sion of our epoch.

From this one passes readily to the point of Spinoza's
remark that "the free man thinks of nothing less than
of death," a remark to be cherished all the more in a
world so full of death in which eschatology is the
fashionable word of the moment. "The free man's

wisdom is a meditation not of death but of life,"—so Spinoza continues this memorable saying,—and to break the habits of the recent past one might begin by reading the great authors who celebrate equally life and man. Why dwell on the death-obsessed John Donne, or John Dryden either, that other literary favourite of the post-war years, both poets of disillusion and reaction whose vogue has been one of the moral symptoms of the time? And why not read more of St. Francis and less of St. Augustine, whose *Confessions* has been so popular in this generation and who has confirmed a general belief that evil and sin, for religion, are a great deal more important than goodness and love? Why not return to Plutarch, too, whom everybody read in the days when people studied beauty of conduct and when they selected from the past whatever corroborated their own mood, or what they desired for a mood, the heroic and the noble? Is it so much better to select from the past the writers who merely endorse the general contemporary feeling of the paltriness of men, Pascal and Machiavelli, for instance, contemners of human nature both, with a shrewd eye for hypocrisy, the wicked and the mean? Is even the "sublime misanthrope" Pascal a better reporter of the nature of man than Rabelais who chose *Fay ce que vouldras* as the motto of his abbey, assuming that men who were properly taught would wish to do nothing inhumane and would naturally shun vice and tend towards virtue? All praise to Rabelais' "honour system" and faith in human decency, which anticipated the thinkers of the revolutionary epoch; and let no one disparage the Renaissance which first deployed for modern men the treasures of the mind in literature and art. Or the Enlightenment, either, with its belief in the dignity of men, which has given them the courage and the strength to develop the world in the face of authoritarian systems that have dwelt on their worthlessness and the meaninglessness of all their strivings for happiness and health.

So much for the diagnostic writers, and so much for the curative,—to return to the definition of Ezra Pound,—the curative writers like Dickens and Balzac, or Molière, for another, who communicate positive feelings and confidence in life. There is *The Good Earth,* too, the world novel of Pearl Buck, a universal book of our own time, which conveys, in characters with whom words have their full weight, a sense of the basic integrities on which societies are built. Then there is Trollope, a Philistine, but who does not relish robustness after the peevish airs of the precious of today, as one relishes Rubens's earthiness after too long an immersion in the thin blood of abstract art? Who, for the rest, does not relish in Trollope the clear sense of right and wrong that our novelists seem to have lost and will have to regain, if they are to count once more in life and letters, the wish to "make virtue alluring and vice ugly" to the reader, whom the novelist charms in the act of doing this? * Who would

* "It is not for the novelist to say, baldly and simply, 'Because you lied here, or were heartless there, because you Lydia Bennet forgot the lessons of your honest home, or you Earl Leicester were false through your ambition, or you Beatrix

wish to banish the diagnostic writers, as Plato banished the poets from his republic? But should they be accorded the dominant place which they have assumed in our day?—should they be permitted to eclipse the curative writers? I suggest that we need above all at present those who can restore for us a feeling for the true aims of living, who can remind us of the goodness in men, bring back the joy of life and give one a sense of human hope. For "what proof is there," said William James, "that dupery through hope is so much worse than dupery through fear?" For another matter, I suggest that we should think less of immature people and more of the developed people we wish to be or we would abolish our schools and our civilization; and I suggest that we should cease to read the critics who analyze, in favour of those who synthesize or bring things together. By these I mean the Sainte-Beuves and De Quinceys, even the James Russell Lowells, who reveal the fruitful interaction of literature and life. I would further suggest an hour of silence regarding Melville and Henry James before they have been killed for all time with kindness.

Nor would I stop there. I would insist on the defence of culture against the reversion to barbarism that is in fashion, against the Rimbauds of our time who greet with a loud *merde!* all references to writers and

loved too well the glitter of the world, therefore you shall be scourged with scourges either in this world or in the next'; but it is for him to show, as he carries on his tale, that his Lydia, or his Leicester, or his Beatrix, will be dishonoured in the estimation of all readers by his or her vices."—Anthony Trollope, *Autobiography*.

artists who are outside their clique. I would insist on the speaking of the words that stand for all we value most,—courage, love, tenderness, happiness, hope and trust,—against the absurd contemporary fear of using words and naming names or what Hemingway calls "talking a lot of rot." What Hawthorne said of the old New Englanders, that *because they did not talk* they might well some day *cease to feel* may prove to be still more true in our dead-pan hard-boiled world that thinks "you'll lose it if you talk about it." Does not every woman know that love grows with the expression of it and that love, no longer mentioned, dies? Do not all the good things similarly grow the more they exist in our consciousness and the more, up to a point, we talk about them?—and, after our tight-lipped recent past, can we really hear too much of the sentiments and the feelings that make us men? Because great words have been used too loosely, are we not to use great words at all? Because we believe in semantics must we be dumb? And are we to be frightened away from expressing and extolling the positive and the good because of the adolescent embarrassment of certain writers who have accepted the notion of the "escape from feeling" that has made modern poetry so frigid and so sterile? For the rest, when all sentiment, true or false, is banned from poetry and prose alike, the distinction between true and false has ceased to be apparent, and every expression of feeling now is described as "sentimental," especially feeling for anything one happens not to like. For nothing could be more sentimental than much current writing about matadors, bar-tenders, Baudelaire and Henry James. Let us restore the prestige of the despised Robert Cohn, the young man in *The Sun Also Rises,* who behaved so badly, from the point of view of his little set, because he had the courage to admit his feelings.

In short, let us put an end to the "cult of callousness," as Lewis Mumford calls it,—the insensitive, the brutal,—that cult of immaturity, good for blustering boys alone, which is really based on nothing but the fear of life. We have heard too much of Nietzsche's injunction, "Be hard!"; and there is nothing less unmanly than the injunction, "Be gentle!"—nothing that more certainly indicates maturity and strength. Would the followers of Hemingway who delight in blood call Mark Twain a sissy because he grieved over a bird that a hunter had crippled and because he wrote a moving tale about an old horse in the bull-ring to express his virile disgust for this low sport? Is it a sign of maturity to repress one's sensibilities and even, by fostering the impassive, to reject all feelings, or rather to develop these and cultivate one's sympathies to the point of reverencing life, in Schweitzer's phrase? When Schweitzer extended this so far as to say we should save the lives of earthworms,—as Gandhi, in his cult of nonviolence towards living creatures, was careful to preserve the silk-worms that were diseased, transferring them to a place where they could thrive,—when Schweitzer and Gandhi went so far they only carried to the extreme the best of possible practices for the cause of life-enhancement. And for the cause of happiness, too, which ought to displace in our minds the cause and the cult of suffering that flourish today, a day in which merely to be unhappy is taken for a sign of grace, as something that indicates goodness and the way of the saints. Do we not know that Nazism was built on the cult of suffering, on the wish *not* to believe that war could be abolished or that disaster and pain would ever cease? At a time when so many legitimately suffer, one cannot be surprised that this mystique of masochism should have spread through the world. But no more than callousness or hardness does it signify goodness. To refer to William James again, his *Varieties of Religious Experience* surveys and describes the minds of many saints, concluding that "there is an organic affinity between joyousness and tenderness": the saints are not hard or sad,—they are "joyous and tender."

What is true of the saints, moreover, is generally true of human life inasmuch as happiness and goodness are one and the same, to such an extent that an old English bishop said, "If it were not so difficult, virtue would hardly be distinguishable from a kind of sensuality." Did not St. Augustine agree with this when he remarked, "Act we must in pursuance of that which gives us most delight"?—and the burden of all the great works of literature, if Matthew Arnold is not mistaken, has always been the desire that the good may prevail. Even in our nihilistic day writers must feel that this is true, whether or not they respond to negation with the faith of eschatology, or what Evelyn Waugh calls a "stampede to the heights." These heights are the "four last things," death, judgment, heaven and hell, the stakes of Pascal's wager, which fill many minds at present, while others, equally sincere, prefer to say with Thoreau,—as long as we are living on this planet,—"One world at a time." And this world also has its heights, to be reached not by stampeding but by a slow painful groping march. Those who deny the reality of progress have never pictured to themselves the caves in which all men lived a few thousand years ago, quarreling over bones and bits of deerskin; and those who identify the world with the expedient and the useful alone have never conceived the idea of *"another world" in this one*. Progress is not a mere matter of high wages and sanitation, although, for the matter of that, is the material to be despised so long as "indigence is the death of the soul,"—as George Gissing said,—and for hundreds of millions of men indigence is wealth? Charles Péguy observed, "No man can be saved from mental or moral misery so long as he is not saved from economic destitution," implying that Christianity necessitates economic justice; and he who despises the notion of progress as merely material ignores the fact that the material and the spiritual are not unconnected. Insecurity and fear destroy the soul likewise; and the abolition of all these evils is the great half-conscious aim of the wars of religion, or "ideology," that harry us today. But without this universal *mêlée* could "one world" ever come about? Without general war could there ever be general peace?—a question that leads to the further question, If the world survives this general war, will anyone doubt in future the reality of progress? For then war will be seen as a necessary step in the long evolutionary process in which it is apparent already, as Bertrand Russell says, that forethought more and more dominates impulse, while only a few generations have passed since whole races of men regarded one another as animals or devils. The fact of progress is evident enough in a world that is emerging from the tribal state, even in epochs like our own when Reversion drags Evolution in the mud, as Herman Melville said in one of his poems.

What has made progress possible has been the wish to transform the world, the opposite of the wish to renounce it as an illusion, as vain, as merely a vestibule to some other world, as something predestined to ruin or to pass like a dream in the night, unworthy of our interest. And what has made possible this positive wish has been a belief in life and man as incomparably important and valuable, to be treasured and cherished,—in life as something to be maintained, affirmed, promoted, revered, enhanced, in man as indefinitely improvable but inherently decent. This view of man and life is fitting for Americans, who cannot sincerely think of the world as finished and for whom it is natural to share a philosophy that favours the advance of humankind against everything that limits or injures or inhibits or destroys it. In the long run, in fact, if civilization survives our time, which view *must* prevail, the affirmative or the negative vision,—that vision which is gambling on the end of the world and seeking to escape from it, as desperate sailors escape from a sinking ship? It is true that the world may well go down in some atomic war. There is perhaps an even chance of this. But, if it does not go down, the history of our race will have just begun,—our civilization will stand at 12:01 in the morning. For we have had only five thousand years of this and mankind's life-expectancy is several million years. There is no less reason, for the rest, to suppose that a great new epoch is about to begin than that the world has reached the end of its tether; and, if this proves to be true, the unconscious that governs the collective literary mind will undergo a momentous alteration. When Faulkner, saying in his Stockholm speech, "I decline to accept the end of man," added that man will not merely "endure" but "prevail," he expressed a faith that is borne out in few of his own writings and in few other novelists and poets of our time. But if writers could break the evil spell that weighs upon their minds they would write fully in that faith, if I am not mistaken, for they would then be astride again of the instincts that are natural to them and that are paralyzed at present. It seems to me likely, in spite of appearances, that, in some future not too remote, we may look for some such transformation. For that way lies the line of human growth.

# INDEX

# INDEX

# Date Due